For Kylie, Taylor, Emily, and Jessica

Contents

Introduction 3

The Purpose of Government 14

The Legislative Branch......................................18

The Executive Branch..25

The Judicial Branch..30

The Rights of the Citizen 37

Amendment I 45

Amendments II-IV...53

Amendments V-VIII...63

Amendments IX & X..77

Economic Systems..84

Ecclesial versus Secular Interests....................92

Women in American 101

International Relations...................................109

Conclusion 120

A Note from the Author..................................123

Works Cited..126

Introduction

We the People. In just these three words, the Founding Fathers set forth what would be the basis for democracy in the United States. But, more than 200 years have passed since these words were written in our Constitution. Could it be possible that more than 200 years later, we no longer abide by these words?

When America declared her independence, the Continental Army still had to fight for another six years to break Britain's chains of tyranny. Even today, tyranny is still a concept which we Americans speak of with fear. Could it be that as a result of our fear of tyranny, the American people have oppressed themselves?

Of course, the average American does not actively seek to vote against themselves, but so many of our political establishments are founded on principals that keep as much political power as possible out of the hands of American voters.

One thing that Americans take for granted is the level of efficiency at which our political system works. Simply, many citizens are operating on the idea that our political system does not need to be fixed, because it is operating the way it always has. However, many people would argue-and probably make a strong case- that the system is broken. In many ways, both of these sentiments are correct.

The idea that our political system is working as it always has and the idea that our system is "broken" would be considered equally true by many. What happened to the three words by which tyranny is thwarted? What happened to *We the People*?

One of the foremost problems facing our ability for self-government is how uneducated the American populace is on what is actually stated in the Constitution. Although the vast majority of Americans patriotically support what is embodied in the Constitution, very few of them have actually read it. In fact, a 2010 survey showed that although nearly all Americans support what is stated in the Constitution, only 79% say that they actually understand at least part of the constitution, and only 28% have read the entire constitution; this number is higher among older generations, and lower within the ranks of younger Americans[1].

This problem is bigger than a few apathetic

individuals who do not take initiative to study our charter of government. This blood lies on the hands of our government itself. One of the responsibilities that federal and state governments collaborate on is the responsibility of educating America's youth. In this way, the government is responsible for making sure that the public is educated on this most important document.

This responsibility is taken somewhat lightly by the school boards that set forth curricula. To put it in the wise words of former President, George W. Bush, "Rarely is the question asked, is our children learning?" Humorous as these words may be, we often take for granted that our nation's youth are being taught about government. In fact, only one in ten American students has adequate knowledge on the system of checks and balances in the Constitution, and three-quarters of high school seniors in 2011 could not name a single power that the Constitution grants to Congress[2].

One of the reasons that so many people may say that our political system is both running as it always has and also broken is because their lack of constitutional knowledge doesn't allow them to conceptualize how smoothly our political system flows.

But, a lack of constitutional knowledge can be dangerous. If the average citizen does not know the confines of government, then that government is due to break free from its cage and suppress the rights of the people. Should the United States reach this point, there will be no return. In this country, all change must be effected by the majority, and the unknowing majority will speak louder than the knowing minority.

Today, it seems that popular politics is more about party affiliation, name-calling, and fear mongering than it is about effecting change, platform, or accountability. The Founding Fathers operated under the principal that virtually no change could be for the worst that was effected by the people. However, did the Founding Fathers expect that so few people would take it upon themselves to learn which rights are afforded to them by the law of the land?

Although people may not know all the minutia of the Constitution, they know their rights. Sure, people may not know the structure of our government, and sure, hardly a third of people can name the three branches of government[3], but they know when their rights are being infringed. This reality, though somewhat bitter, is not entirely unforeseen.

To many, politics is something that is only important once every four years in a city far away from where they live. On the other hand, citizens exercise the rights that the Constitution ensures, especially those enumerated in the Bill of Rights, every day. Every day Americans rely on their ability to speak, assemble, and worship freely. So, keeping in mind that most Americans fervently uphold their rights, despite their limited knowledge on the document that gives them, we must ask: *Could the government get away with exploiting lack of constitutional knowledge to take rights away?* In all honesty, probably not.

The very nature of the system of checks and balances is what makes it possible for the average Joe to feel comfortable enough to only vote once every four years without the fear that those in power are conspiring to take away his unalienable rights. If a government is stable, it has no interest in taking away rights from its citizens. However, if a nation is not in a state of stability, the following conditions allow for the usurpation of rights by the government without insurrection by the people.

1. Generally, the ruling power will only take rights away from the people when the situation is so dire that unalienable rights seem like a fair trade for stability.

Take as an example Germany's Weimar Republic, the government implemented in 1919 that eventually gave rise to Hitler in 1933. During this period, Germany was ordered to pay France about $12.5 billion (USD) that they simply did not have as reparations for World War I.

In response, Germany just decided to print the money that it needed. Obviously, this led to disastrous consequences for Germany such as inflation, supply shortages, and devaluation of their dollar. In fact, it is even said that inflation was so bad that if one were to purchase a coffee, in the time between waiting in line and paying, the coffee would have doubled in price due to the rampant inflation.

Enter charismatic politician, Adolf Hitler. While the fiscal situation in Germany was a bubble due to burst at any moment, it is easy to see how Hitler was able to seduce the nation with his talk of restoration. When Hitler's Nazi party finally gained power, he began infringing on Germans' rights by taking away their guns, but the Germans didn't mind, as they saw the wheels of progress beginning to turn.

2. Usually an already disliked minority is offered as a scapegoat for the misfortunes that the nation has suffered.

Going along with the previous example of Hitler's Germany, his scapegoat was quite obvious. Hitler blamed Jewish people and Communists for the bulk of Germany's problems. At this time, many Germans were taught in religious schools that Jewish people were inferior to Christians. Many German people also had never met a Jewish person, as the Jewish population was concentrated in large cities. It is easy to discern why so many Germans could be convinced that the Jewish populace was the root of their problems.

Similarly, the Armenians were put into this position during World War I. Because the people of the Ottoman Empire- largely Muslim- had already been suspicious of the Christian Armenians, the

Young Turks were easily able to convince the Ottomites that the Christian Armenians were conspiring to take Istanbul. As a result of extreme anti-Armenian propaganda, the Turks were able to exterminate 1.5 million Armenians while the majority of the population was left feeling safer. Interestingly enough, despite the best efforts of Kim Kardashian, the Turkish government still denies that this genocide takes place[4].

3. The movement to take rights away is usually proposed by a radical faction operating under unchecked power.

We are all familiar with the James Madison quote that states:

> "If angels were to govern men, neither external nor internal controls on government would be necessary. In framing a government which is to be administered by men over men, the great difficulty lies in this: you must first enable the government to control the governed; and in the next place, oblige it to control itself."

As the father of our constitution, it is evident how Madison used these words as a precedent in his writings. In the United States, our three branches of government are limited by checks and balances. If a radical faction were to come to power in one of the three branches, the other two are obligated to control this threat by using checks and balances in order to ensure it does not overstep its bounds. But outside of the government, the people are the most important agent in controlling tyranny.

One interesting phenomenon that naturally occurs in the United States is that when the President is of one party, citizens vote to put the other party in Congress. Furthermore, when the presidency changes parties, the midterm congressional election is of the upmost importance, as this is the first opportunity for the electorate respond to the new president and check his power by putting the other political party into power.

This equalizing method is best shown in the transition of power from President George H. W. Bush to President Clinton. Because Bush was a Republican, he left behind a Democrat-heavy congress. When Clinton won the Presidency, he inherited this liberal congress. However, in the 1994 congressional mid-term elections, the American people elected Republicans into both houses of his congress[5]. This is a way in which the American people prevent one of the political parties from becoming too powerful.

Historically speaking, these three criterion reoccur whenever a governing body is successful in taking rights away from its citizens. With due diligence of American citizens and the competitive system of checks and balances, it is unforeseeable that a mass exodus of unalienable rights could occur in the United States.

Although our inalienable rights have been the same since they were enumerated in the Declaration of Independence by Thomas Jefferson and the Committee of Five, our Constitution has changed much since its ratification.

In the past 230 years that the United States has been a country, our nation has expanded, progressed, and advanced. Despite how far we have come, our Constitution has only been amended 17 times (excluding the Bill of Rights, which was proposed the same year that the Constitution was ratified). In the face of so much change, our Constitution has been stretched to its limits and forced to extents that the Framers themselves would have been incapable of predicting.

Although it is true that the United States has evolved, the same can not necessarily be said for the Constitution. Our most important plan for government is rarely amended, however it is consulted with most every piece of legislation passed and court case heard. Because of the unwavering nature of our Constitution, we frequently have to make inferences about the Framer's intent. Although documents such as *The Federalist Papers* can help us determine this intent, situations regularly arise that require us to take license in interpreting the Constitution.

The Federal Government today is much more integrated into our lives than it was the lives of the revolutionary generation. Even with this vast amount of expansion, we have kept the same Constitution. Any successful Constitution is written with a degree of flexibility, in order to allow continuous governance in a world of constant change. While the United States Constitution is incredibly flexible, it is not infinitely so. Our Constitution has had to bend and stretch at many junctions in our nation's history. While it is necessary for a nation's laws to progress with the nation itself, the Constitution is not able to do the same. So can we really say that the Constitution is evolving? Or is it perhaps devolving into something that the Framers never wanted.

James Madison, the father of the Constitution, once said:

> "Freedom has more often been lost in small steps by progressive incrementalism, than it has been by catastrophic upheavals such as violence or war"

Although the functions of the Federal Government are vastly different now than they were in James Madison's time, these changes did not happen suddenly. Gradually, our government appropriated roles that it was originally not supposed to play. As the needs of citizens expand, the government must likewise expand. However, is this expansion for the best?

References

1. Fitzgerald, Sharon C., Daily Progress Correspondent. "Survey: U.S. Admires, but Hasn't Read, Constitution." *The Daily Progress*. 23 Jan. 2013. Web. 12 February 2016.

2. Hentoff, Nat. "Our Constitution: How Many of Us Know It?" *Cato Institute*. 19 May 2011. Web. 12 February 2016.

3. Wilson, Reid. "Only 36 Percent of Americans Can Name the Three Branches of Government." *The Washington Post*. 18 September 2014. Web. 27 February 2016.

4. Adalian, Rouben Paul. "Turkey, Republic of, and the Armenian Genocide." *Armenian National Institute*. N.D. Web. 6 March 2016.

5. The Federal Election Commission. *Federal Election 94: Election Results for the U.S. Senate and the U.S. House of Representatives*. (Washington D.C. 1995) Pages 7-30.

The Purpose of Government

One of the foremost responsibilities of government is to set forth laws for society and ensure that they are followed. The laws that are implemented by the government are put forth because they protect liberties at the expense of giving up rights. This concept of the social contract is nothing new, it has been a prominent topic in philosophy since the early 17th century.

In American philosophical thought, the models of the social contract by Jean-Jacques Rousseau and John Locke are the ones that we think of the most, because they are the closest to our own system of government. Locke and Rousseau state that when citizens collectively give up rights, the state absorbs those rights and in turn has an obligation to maintain the liberties of the collective. Our constitution echoes this thought at the end of the preamble when it states that one of its goals is to "secure the blessings of liberty".

In order to truly understand how ingrained the idea of the social contract is in our government, we must compare ourselves to the state of nature. The state of nature is a hypothetical condition which philosophers such as Thomas Hobbs, John Locke, Montesquieu, and Jean-Jacques Rousseau have used to represent a society with no government at all. In this society, no crime exists because there is no governing body to interpret right from wrong. In a state of nature, everybody would retain the ability to murder without consequence, simply because there is no governing body to punish those who take life. In the United States (as well as most other countries) murder is a crime. Because of this, people give up the ability to murder in exchange for the government protecting their right to life. Should somebody commit murder, the government would be obligated by the social contract to punish them for violating somebody's right to life.

This theory of the social contract also plays into what we will call the theory of net good. This theory is simply based on the idea of doing the most amount of good for as many people as possible. *Maximum good.* This means that when drafting laws, Congress needs to look at what would be in the best interest of the most people. With the previous example of murder, it is probably in the best interest of all people to have their right to life protected.

However, this concept of net good is not always as clear cut as the last example made it out to be. Take for example, one of the most controversial acts to be passed in a generation: The Affordable Care Act. If we use the theory of maximum good, then the most obvious stance on the Affordable Care Act is that the most good is done when as many people as possible have access to affordable healthcare coverage. Although this act positively impacted the lives of 20 million Americans[1], the other component of maximum good is that as many people as possible must benefit. The most valid argument against Obamacare is that it causes insurance premiums to go up for those that do not qualify for Obamacare.

This presents a conundrum for the theory of net good. Although the previously uninsured 20 million gain much from this act, does that make up for all those paying for these benefits? The burden of paying for this premium falls on the shoulders of many more than 20 million people. So the question is this: which takes precedent: how much good is being done? Or how many people are benefitting?

Those who are in support of Obamacare would raise the argument that the amount of good is more important. Because of Obamacare, more than 12 million Americans now have coverage that did not previously[2]. Without a doubt, these peoples' lives have changed because now they enjoy the ability to get treated for medical conditions, allowing them to enjoy a higher quality of life than before. Obamacare also serves as an equalizing mechanism between the rich and the poor. Without access to healthcare, the poor would inevitably not be as healthy as the wealthy, which would ultimately lead to lower life expectancies for the less fortunate. However, Obamacare does not help the majority of Americans.

Those who are opposed to Obamacare focus on those that are not helped by the act, rather than those who benefit from it. This side of the argument focuses on the fact that there are more Americans paying for Obamacare than there are Americans benefitting from Obamacare. Many opponents to the program do not believe that the current healthcare system is without flaws, but rather, they disagree with where money for the program comes from.

This is the problem with the theory of net good, what takes precedent? The amount of people who benefit? Or how much better the lives of those who benefit become? Every day in Washington DC, our legislators are faced with the impossible task of deciding who gets to benefit, how much, and more importantly: who does not. This is why the powers of the legislative branch could not be concentrated into one person, or even one house.

-The Legislative Branch-

To put it in the simplest terms, the job of the legislature is to write new laws or make changes to old laws. At the federal level of the United States, the legislature is split into the two houses of Congress with which we are familiar: the Senate and the House of Representatives. For the most part, the duties of these two houses are very similar, but they each have distinct duties that play a significant part in their responsibilities to the American people.

When our Constitution was first ratified, and for 125 years thereafter, the House of Representatives was the only federal entity elected directly by the people. In this way, the House of Representatives has the richest history of being directly accountable to the people of the United States. This claim is also supported by the fact that in the House, the Representatives are directly responsible for campaigning the interests of their district.

Furthermore, the representatives are up for reelection every two years- as opposed to every six for senators. Because representatives are frequently up for reelection, they must be responsive to the will of the people in order to ensure their reelection. And, because of its larger size, the House is generally considered to be the more partisan chamber. However, this isn't necessarily a bad thing, these differences in opinion allow representatives from every corner of the country to hear the beliefs of Americans from all walks of life. This is what allows for national tolerance and understanding. In addition, the smaller size of the Senate naturally lends itself to more clear-cut solutions, rather than the compromises that naturally come to fruition in the House due to the wide array of interests represented there.

Because the House of Representatives has such a deep legacy of directly promoting the interests of the people that it represents, it has special powers reserved to it. The most important of these responsibilities is that the House is responsible for electing the President in the event that no presidential candidate reaches 270 electoral votes. In the event that the House has to elect the president (an occurrence which has not happened since 1824) each state only receives one vote.

This is one of the idiosyncrasies in the House of Representatives. The founding ideal of the House is that all of the diverse interests within a state are not homogenized, but rather are given their fair share of representation. In addition, this is blatantly unfair to states with large populations. Because of this provision, the representatives of California and Wyoming both get one vote in selecting the president, despite the fact that California's population is more than 66 times greater than Wyoming's[3]. Not only was this provision was not one of the terms in the Connecticut compromise, it goes against this compromise altogether.

The responsibility of the House of Representatives is to be responsive to the issues, beliefs, and concerns of their district. In the event that the House of Representatives has to select the President, can the House actually fulfill this responsibility? To the best of their abilities, the representatives can, as long as they cast their ballot in favor of whichever candidate the majority of their constituents support. However, it is not fair that a resident of Wyoming should receive 66 times the amount of direct representation as a person in California in this situation. Whether or not the members of the House of Representatives find this provision fair, it is something that they must act on, should the need be.

Something that the House does have more control over, however, is levying taxes. In Article I, Section 7 of the constitution, all rights to propose bills on raising revenue are reserved to the House of Representatives. The Framers took this concept right from the provisions of England's parliamentary system. In Britain, all "money bills" must originate in the House of Commons[4], because it is the more representative of the two houses of Parliament. This is one of the areas that makes the best use of the House's representative abilities.

Whereas senators must represent their state as a whole, representatives represent a select geographic area (with the exception of the seven states that only have one representative). The residents of a certain district are not only bound by their place of residence, they usually consist of groups with similar beliefs, socio-economic levels, and cultures. Each Representative plays just one part in representing the vast interests of every citizen in the United States. This is where the House's ability for reaching compromises proves useful. Because representatives are expected to advocate for all types of people, compromise is inevitable. Each group gains some benefits and is in turn expected to give up some of their original wishes in order to promote the general welfare.

The founding principal of the United States' legislative system is that two types of diversity are represented: diversity by population and diversity of states. Diversity by population can be associated with the House of Representatives because representation is given in direct proportion to the population of a state. However, diversity of the states is an equally important factor to consider when speaking about representation. If representation were only given based on population size, it would only take the nine most populous states voting the same way to disenfranchise the other 41 states. These states with higher populations also tend to have more people living in urban areas than the less populated states. This means that if representation were based on population alone, urban interests would almost always win out over rural or agrarian ones.

To maximize the impact of diversity by

population and diversity of states, the Constitution makes use of the Connecticut Compromise. The Connecticut Compromise is what separates our legislature into the House of Representatives and the Senate. The Senate is the part of Congress responsible for maintaining diversity of the states.

Unlike the representatives, senators are not responsible for representing a single area of their state, but rather their state as a whole. This is part of the reason that Senators are elected for longer terms than representatives. Representatives are elected more frequently in order to make them more receptive to the popular sentiment of the area that they represent. However, the Framers were concerned that what was popular at any given moment may not be beneficial to the nation in the long term. In order to balance popular passions with long-term sustainability, the Framers gave senate members longer terms.

With the advice and consent of the Senate, the President is given the authority to make treaties. Many of the treaties that go through the Senate deal with relations with foreign countries, which is usually something that the President handles alone, however during the constitutional convention, Charles Pinckney argued that the Senate should be the only body capable of making treaties, because it is there that each state is equally represented. To this, Alexander Hamilton responded that the ability to exercise powers related to foreign nations should remain with the President, but treaties drafted by the President should be approved by the Senate[5]. This responsibility was reserved to the Senate rather than the House of Representatives because foreign relations affect every state, demographic, and area of the country equally. As with any issue that will have an equal impact on every citizen, it is important that the Senate has the final say, because it is in the Senate that every state is allowed to have equal input.

In the respect of leadership, the Senate is also far different from the House of Representatives. The House is characterized by having a stronger, internal system of leadership where power is concentrated in the Speaker and the Speaker's advisors. Power is more evenly split among members of the Senate, which has a weaker system of leadership, due in part to its small size. Sustainability is key in the Senate. The rules of the Senate ensure that the solutions reached will be beneficial for the nation in the present and in the future. This is why in the Senate, the rules for floor debate are very loose, and debate limits are very rare. In the house, scheduling is controlled by the majority party and the strict debate rules favor the majority party. The rules (or lack thereof) in the Senate allow for equal input from both political parties, which lends itself to the more clear-cut solutions that characterize decisions made by the Senate.

In the interest of sustainability, the Senate also is not allowed to create ad hoc committees

(committees created for a particular issue and subsequently disbanded when the issue is resolved). In the House, ad hoc committees are created at the discretion of the Speaker. As a result of this, members of the House are usually more specialized in the interests they advocate for. In the Senate, members are usually more general in regards to their advocacy.

The generality found in the Senate also lends itself to foreign policy decisions. If foreign policy decisions were concentrated in the House, rather than the senate, the specialization of interests would not lead to cohesive nor sustainable solutions. However, this breadth of interests and depth of knowledge does prove useful when making tax and revenue policy, a responsibility primarily designated to the House.

The Founding Fathers intended on making the legislative branch the most important branch of our government. Consequently, they reserved the most important power of governance to Congress: the power to make laws. This power is split across the two houses that make up Congress; although similar in nature, the slight differences between these houses allow them to serve our nation in slightly different capacities.

-The Executive Branch-

Article II of the Constitution lays forth the duties of the Executive Branch of the government. This branch is headed by the President and employs the most people out of the three branches (4.4 million when uniformed military personnel are counted[6]).

When the Framers first created the office of the President, they did not intend for the President to have much real power- but rather to act as a check on the authority of Congress. Those who were in favor of having a strong President often were censured by the label *monarchist*. When the Framers first created this office, they were satisfied in themselves for creating a position with much prestige, but little real authority.

The presidency has evolved with time into the strong position that it is today. Ever since the days of Washington, each President has played a role in expanding the role of the Presidency. George Washington was the first to invoke executive privilege when he refused to share documents with Congress about the Jay Treaty. Further down the line, Andrew Jackson was the first President to extensively use veto power, vetoing more bills than all the six presidents before him combined[7]. Abraham Lincoln would be the next President to substantially expand the powers of the executive office.During the Civil War, President Lincoln loosely interpreted his abilities as commander-in-chief of the armed forces in order to expand his capabilities as President. At the turn of the 20th century, Theodore Roosevelt made use of one of the most powerful tools for the expansion of presidential power: public opinion.

Theodore Roosevelt referred to the presidency as a "bully pulpit" which could be utilized to shape public opinion in his favor. The executive office is well-designed for this, as its power is concentrated into just one central figure: the President. The President is just one person, with one public policy, and one agenda to advertise to the American people. Compare this to the hundreds of members of Congress, each with his or her own ideas, policies, and agendas, and it is easy to see why the President is more effective in shaping American public opinion than Congress.

The media has also helped facilitate the expansion of the President's power via public opinion. Since the first televised presidential debate between presidential candidates Nixon and Kennedy in 1960, oratorical abilities have had the ability to make or break a president's reception. In fact, the 1960 debates proved that the days of presidential anonymity were long gone. In the 1960 debate, television viewers reported that calm, cool, and collected Kennedy had won over a visibly anxious Nixon. However, when radio listeners were polled about the victor of the debate, the majority said that

Nixon had won.

The assertion that public perception is becoming increasingly important is substantiated by the list of our Presidents with outstanding aptitudes for public speaking. This list includes Presidents Andrew Jackson, Abraham Lincoln, Franklin Roosevelt, John F. Kennedy, Ronald Reagan, Bill Clinton, and Barack Obama. Many of these Presidents served recently and were broadcast on the airwaves to the American people. However, this increase in communication is not just contained within the borders of our country.

As the world opens more international channels of communication, the role of the presidency further expands. Because it is easier for foreign countries to conduct affairs with only one person, rather than the entirety of Congress, the Constitution grants most of the powers pertaining to foreign relations to the President. In this age, communication and travel are instantaneous, even on a global scale. With more frequent interaction between nations, the President's role naturally expands. Now, the President is no longer the figurehead, or the check on Congress that James Madison intended, but rather something that the Framers might see as "monarchist".

One of the original powers that the Framers *did* grant to the President, however, is veto power. The official job of the President is to "execute" the laws, which essentially means that his office is the last stop for bills before they are enacted as laws. The President may veto laws after they are approved by Congress, but one of the checks that the Legislature has over the Presidency is the power to overturn the veto with a 2/3 vote.

When the Framers first wrote this into the Constitution, they didn't have to deal with strong political parties that we have today. Many modern political scholars argue that the Presidency has become more powerful because of the partisan politics that dominate in Congress. Although it is attainable for half of the members of Congress to pass a bill, it is much less likely that 2/3 of them will vote in the manner needed to overturn a Presidential veto. So even if a party has a majority in Congress, enough to pass a bill on to the President, it is unlikely that the party will have 2/3 of both houses (in fact this has not happened since the Congressional elections of 1964). So, overturning a Presidential veto requires quite a bit of straddling across party lines on the part of Congress, making this process nearly impossible in the political binary that our system is based in today.

Not only does political gridlock stall an already slow system, it strengthens an office that the Framers intended to be weak. While much of the expansion of the presidency is due to the increasing demands of the job, the presidency should not be expanding due to political conflict in another branch of government. Organically, the only way that the Presidency should be able to grow is if the demands on the office increase.

Historically, the President has always been the face of America- both at home and abroad. But the demands on the President to carry out his duties in the area of foreign relations has never been greater. While the President has always been chief diplomat for the United States, this role is more important now than ever in our history. Time has taken the office of the President from a figurehead position to one of great authority.

-The Judicial Branch-

The Judicial Branch is the branch of government that is responsible for interpreting and exercising the law of the United States. At the head of the Judicial Branch is the Supreme Court of the United States. This court has the responsibility of making sure that all laws enacted in the United States are Constitutional, and do not infringe on any of the rights that citizens retain.

However, the Constitution does not grant the Supreme Court the power of judicial review. In *Federalist No. 78*[8], Alexander Hamilton describes the process of judicial review, saying that Congress itself cannot be trusted to uphold the Constitution in each of the laws that it passes. But, the real precedent for judicial review was established in the Supreme Court case *Marbury v. Madison*[9]. In this case, Supreme Justice John Marshall declared that the Judiciary Act of 1789 was unconstitutional, and that furthermore, it is up to the Supreme Court to decide what the Constitution permits.

Out of articles I, II, and III, (respectively the legislative, executive, and judicial articles) the Framers left Article III the shortest. Furthermore, the Constitution does not even grant the Supreme Court the power of judicial review, the ability of the Supreme Court which Americans are most familiar with. In fact, the only powers that are mentioned in

Article III that the Supreme Court retains are the various types of court cases that the Supreme Court has original or appellate jurisdiction in. So we must wonder: *If the Framers did not grant the Supreme Court hardly any powers at all, did they intend for the Judicial Branch to be the weakest branch of our government?*

For all intents and purposes, *yes*. In fact, in *Federalist No. 78*, Alexander Hamilton stated outright that the judicial branch would be the weakest of the three because it would have "no influence over either the sword or the purse ...It may truly be said to have neither FORCE nor WILL, but merely judgment." He contrasts the role of the Supreme Court to that of the President, who retains the right to the sword as commander-in-chief of the armed forces, and to that of Congress, which is responsible for levying taxes. Hamilton then goes on to say that the Supreme Court has only the power of judgement over the other two branches, making it the weakest of the branches. It is in the best interest of the citizens of the United States if the Supreme Court does not hold the power to raise taxes or command the army. Any additional responsibilities that the court has further opens it up to the possibility of conflicts of interest.

But, although this branch is the weakest, it serves one of the most important functions out of all the three branches: it ensures that the Constitution is being upheld, despite the Framers not originally endowing the Supreme Court with this responsibility.

However, the Framers were not actively trying to seek to keep judicial review out of the court's hands. In fact, state constitutions reveal that a majority of the original 13 states were already practicing judicial review. Furthermore, although the power of judicial review is not explicitly given in the Constitution, all of the provisions in the Constitution lend themselves in a manner that allows judicial review to naturally arise.

Article IV of the Constitution states that the Constitution is the supreme law of the land, and that any laws that are made in conflict with the Constitution are null. Therefore, when any laws or court decisions are made that might conflict with the Constitution, it is the job of the Supreme Court (as the ultimate authority of the land) to interpret the Constitution as it pertains to the situation. Oftentimes, judicial review is called "the great contradiction" because its practice seeks to ensure that the Constitution is being upheld, despite that it itself is not provided for in the Constitution.

The judiciary system in the United States is what provides us with the right to a fair and speedy trial. The fifth and sixth amendments provide us with our rights, as they pertain to criminal trials. Under our Constitution, the courts and government are responsible for making sure that our natural rights as citizens are upheld until a jury of impartial peers and due process of laws takes them away.

It is the purpose of the judicial branch to

ensure that the rights of the citizen as laid out in the Constitution are not infringed. And yes, it is true that the judicial branch can lay no claim onto the sword or the purse, but this branch serves as an important check onto the power of the President and Congress. The fact is, Alexander Hamilton was correct; Congress simply cannot be trusted to adhere itself to the rules outlined in the Constitution. In many ways, the judiciary advocates for the rights of the people more than the other two branches, despite the fact that the people have no hand in electing Supreme Court justices at all. So, while the purpose of the judiciary branch is to settle disputes and handle trials, its responsibility to the people is to uphold our unalienable rights while other institutions attempt to take them from us.

The role of government, on the simplest level is to fulfill its place in the social contract opposite the citizens. The citizens depend on the government to protect their rights to life, liberty, and the pursuit of happiness, and to prosecute those who seek to take these rights away from them. When citizens invest their rights into the government in order to make this exchange, they expect that the government is working in their best interest.

James Madison succeeded in his goal of ensuring that the government could control not only the governed, but also itself. Although the three different parts of our government have distinct functions that they perform on a day-to-day basis, our government has stood the test of time because of the checks and balances that oblige the government to control itself.

The ability of the government to control itself is just as important as the ability of the government to control its citizens. So, while it is true that the different functions carried out daily by the three branches are imperative to maintain the social contract, it is checks and balances that ensure long-term stability. In fact, the US Constitution is the oldest written Constitution in the world, despite our nation being in its infancy when compared to other European, African, and Asian countries. So while it is the purpose of Congress to write laws, the President to sign those laws into effect, and the Supreme Court to ensure that those laws are constitutional, each agency has the responsibility of ensuring that the other two do not accumulate too much power.

References

1. Obama, Barack. "Healthy Communities Reward Speech." 3 March 2016. Milwaukee, WI.

2. Congressional Budget Office. "Updated Estimates of the Effects of the Insurance Coverage Provisions of the Affordable Care Act, April 2014." *Congress of the United States Congressional Budget Office.* April 2014. Web. 29 December 2016.

3. The United States Census Bureau. "Annual Estimates of the Resident Population: April 1, 2010 to July 1, 2016." *The United States Census Bureau.* July 2016. 30 December 2016.

4. United Kingdom 1911 Parliament Act. 1911.

5. "The Senate's Role in Treaties." *The United States Senate.* N.D. Web. 3 January 2017.

6. "The Executive Branch." *The White House.* N.D. Web. 22 January 2017.

7. "Vetoes: Summary of Bills Vetoed, 1789-present" *The United States Senate.* N.D. 1 February 2017.

8. Hamilton, Alexander. "Federalist No. 78." The Federalist Papers. 28 May 1788.

9. "Marbury v. Madison." Primary Documents in American History. Library of Congress, n.d. Web. 5 March 2017.

The Rights of the Citizen

In the United States, it is just as true that the people control the government as it is that the government controls the people. While it is also true that the average American only participates in politics once every four years, we are endowed with the right to shape public policy every day. Oftentimes, the people that do take the time to shape public policy are the wealthy, not because they are more virtuous, but rather because they have the means. In fact, out of the top 50 interest groups that give money to members of Congress, only six represent the middle class. The remaining 44 groups represent corporate interests[1].

Simply, most working and middle class Americans do not have the time nor the money to contribute to special interest groups or political action committees. And, while many middle class

Americans are members of labor unions, recently labor unions have been on the decline. Every year the number of people in labor unions decreases, therefore decreasing the ability of labor unions to be a formidable force in shaping opinions in DC.

But, as far as interest groups go, the most underrepresented demographics are those in the lowest income brackets. There are no special interest groups devoted entirely to food stamps, no lobbyists promoting the interests of single mothers, and no political action committees going to work for parents who are forced to mortgage their homes to send their children to college.

Until average citizens take it upon themselves to be more involved in politics, big businesses will continue to speak louder than the majority. The corporate heads of Fortune 500 companies do not have the best interests of average Americans at heart. Therefore, it is up to Americans themselves to ensure that their voice is heard in our expansive nation. In framing the Constitution, the Founding Fathers put down political participation as a right, but it is the responsibility of the citizens to pick up that right and make it work for them.

Of course, voting is the most important civic responsibility in the United States, but so few Americans actually do it on a regular basis. In fact, less than 55% of the voting age population actually cast a vote in the 2012 presidential election[2]. And although this is low, turnout for midterm congressional elections is even lower. The 2014 midterm elections only saw 41.9% of the voting age population cast a ballot[3].

Each election cycle, we hear statistics like this and wonder about the state of our democratic process. Often, these statistics are misleading because they account for populations that aren't even eligible to vote. When only registered voters are taken into consideration (thereby excluding citizens that are eligible to vote, but are not registered) political participation rates go up to almost 65%. Although this is not a staggering improvement, this data reveals the deeper nature of political apathy in the United States. If 65% of registered voters actually vote, then what about the other 35% of registered voters that do not regularly vote? And what of the nearly 80 million American citizens not registered to vote?

In some European and South American nations, voting is compulsory and voter registration forms are filed for each person upon birth. However, in the United States, our first amendment rights do protect, among other things, the freedom of speech and the right of the people to peacefully protest. Some people consider not voting a "protest" against the government and the candidates up for election. Whether or not their premise is valid, the first amendment does protect their right to do this. To that point, there are also Americans who will only vote for a candidate whom they wholeheartedly support: Americans who refuse to choose between the "lesser of two evils". If we make voting compulsory, we make these voters choose to support an agenda with which they do not agree.

Australia, a nation that uses compulsory voting, imposes fines on those who do not vote[4]. In the United States, the Fifth Amendment states that property cannot be taken away without due process of law, meaning that a trial must be offered to non-voters before any fines could be collected. Furthermore, citizens have the right to confront their accuser. When one chooses to go to trial over a speeding ticket, they are able to confront the law enforcement officer who wrote the ticket. *Who would citizens confront in a trial for not voting?* Not only is compulsory voting in the United States against the Constitution, it would require too many resources to be viable.

Although it is our most important civic duty, voting is something that only American citizens can do. For the thousands of permanent residents, who have yet to become a citizen, there are other ways to get involved in politics.

The first amendment gives the right to petition to citizens, but in some circumstances, this right is extended to all. In fact, the website whitehouse.gov is a forum where anyone over the age of 13 can sign a petition. The White House then turns any petitions that gain over 100,000 signatures in a week to the proper committees for consideration. There are still some methods of petitioning in which signatories have to be citizens of a certain district, but this new method of petition opens a door for political involvement of non-citizens.

In most cases, you do not need to be a citizen to call or arrange a meeting with a representative. Calling a Representative is a particularly effective way to get your opinion across, as he or she wants to ensure that the constituents are onboard with new legislation (especially for reelection purposes). And, while it is true that calling a Representative's office will usually get you on the phone with a staffer, these staffers do keep track of how many people call, which issues they wanted to talk about, and their opinion on the issue.

Although these are all ways to get involved in political activities, they only pertain to passing legislation or influencing legislators who already hold office. What about those who want to support a candidate, but cannot vote to do so? One way that anyone can get involved in campaigns is to volunteer or make calls for a political candidate. These opportunities usually come about during the presidential races, but can also be found for senatorial candidates. Making phone calls for a candidate is easy, usually one just calls members of that candidate's party to ensure that they will be voting. The campaign usually provides a script, phone numbers, and basic information about the person, in order to make the process as simple as possible. In presidential campaigns, there are even options to make calls to voters who only speak Spanish.

Although it is important to participate in politics, most Americans do not, except for voting. Even to those who are involved in forms of political participation other than voting, politics is something that is only important every four years, or when they want certain legislation passed. What is important, however, are the rights afforded to us by our Constitution that we use every day.

When the Articles of Confederation failed, the Framers assembled at the Constitutional Convention, originally seeking to amend the Articles. Many of the Framers, most notably James Madison and Alexander Hamilton came with their own agenda: to create an entirely new system for American government. There were still many Framers at the Constitutional Convention that believed in the weak federal government that the Articles of Confederation established. These so-called Antifederalists thought that a strong federal government would lead to tyranny, or worse: monarchy.

In what would become known as the Massachusetts Compromise, the delegates from Massachusetts agreed that they would ratify the Constitution if amendments that reserved rights to the people were added. After hearing about Massachusetts's idea, New York and Virginia promised the same. These amendments would become known as the Bill of Rights, because they enumerate the rights that the citizens of the United

States retain. Today, these amendments still safeguard our rights from those who seek to take or suppress them.

References

1. Wilson, Megan R. "Lobbying's Top 50: Who's Spending Big" *The Hill.* 7 February 2017. Web. 28 May 2016.
2. "Federal Elections 2012: Election Results for the U.S. President, the U.S. Senate, and the U.S. House of Representatives." FEDERAL ELECTIONS 2012 (2013): n. pag. Federal Election Commission. Web.
3. "Who Votes? Congressional Elections and the American Electorate: 1978–2014." Census Bureau, July 2015. Web. 13 June 2016.
4. "Voting within Australia – Frequently Asked Questions." Australian Electoral Commission. N.p., 27 Oct. 2016. Web. 13 June 2016.

Expression
(Amendment I)

The First Amendment is what preserves our freedoms of worship, speech, press, assembly, petition, and peaceful protest. In a land first settled by those seeking escape from religious persecution, the Framers ensured that the tolerant spirit America was founded on would continue. Virtually all of the Framers were of English descent, meaning that the only system of rule that they were familiar with was the English system. According the English way, all political officeholders had to be members of the Anglican Church[1]. Despite the fact that the framers only knew a system of government that used religion as a basis for qualification, they chose not to establish a mandatory religion for officeholders. Religious diversity was already apparent within the Framers themselves. Although all of the Framers were Christians (with the exception of a few deists), they came from different denominations: Catholic, Presbyterian, Dutch Reformed, Baptist, Lutheran, Episcopalian, Congregationalist, and Methodist[2].

Not only does the First Amendment guarantee freedom of religion, it also sets the groundwork for the principal of separation of church and state. In the fourth chapter, the effects of separation of church and state will be further analyzed, but it is this separation that ensures a society where all men are created equal.

The First Amendment also secures freedom of speech, which is one of the rights that Americans hold in the highest esteem. Free speech is one of the most important safeguards against the government becoming too powerful. When grouped with the First Amendment rights to petition and assemble, free speech gives us the right to peacefully protest. Although now any laws that are passed that limit free speech would be declared unconstitutional, the Supreme Court power of judicial review was only established in 1803 because of *Marbury v. Madison.*

In 1798, the Alien and Sedition Acts were passed by President John Adams. The fourth act, the Sedition Act, rendered it illegal to make false statements that were critical of the federal government. When Thomas Jefferson became the President in 1800, one of his first acts was to pardon those serving time under the Sedition Act. The *Marbury v. Madison* case had not yet been seen in the Supreme Court, meaning that judicial review had not been established. This meant that the Sedition Act- which trampled on the right to free speech- was constitutional and enforceable.

Those who were most often prosecuted under the Sedition Act were columnists at newspapers, who printed false statements that were critical of the federal government. So, not only did the Sedition Act go against the principals of free speech, it also went against freedom of the press. Freedom of the press is what enables the public to communicate about abuses of power by the government. If the government were able to control what information reaches the hands of the public, the government would be able to manipulate our democratic institutions themselves.

If the government regulated what went into the news, they would be able to mold public opinion any way that they wanted. The press and other forms of media are the most important component in keeping the government accountable for its actions. With a government-controlled press, the government would not need to report every move they make to the American people, making it easy for them to pass acts without the support of their citizens. This would also mean that if more support were needed to pass an act, lies would be spread in order to gain the support required, and the American public might never know they are being deceived.

Because of freedom of the press, Americans have several news sources to choose from for information. These news sources are constantly in a state of competition with each other to get more readers, viewers, subscribers, etc. Consumers of media want to be updated with breaking news as it happens, causing media outlets to compete with each other to be the first to reveal stories. However, consumers also care about credibility. If a news source gets facts wrong, they will likely lose subscribers. This model of news reporting ensures that the consumers are receiving the most accurate updates as fast as possible. The Framers put freedom of the press into the first amendment because they knew that without the means to freely spread information, the government would not be held accountable for its actions.

Freedom of assembly is also protected under the first amendment. Often, we think of freedom of assembly as being part of freedom of speech, but the two are constituted by different elements. When we think of freedom of assembly, what probably springs to mind is a physical gathering of people. While it is true that these types of gatherings are protected under the first amendment, freedom of assembly extends to other gatherings as well. Union advocates usually cite the freedom to assemble as a protection over their right to unionize.

When the United States was in the midst of revolution, the Founding Fathers were constantly under the threat of being found guilty of conspiracy or treason by the British government. Looking towards the future, they wanted to ensure that freedom of assembly was kept. In the eyes of the Founding Fathers, the ability to assemble, especially to discuss the nature of government should not be limited.

The freedom to peacefully petition goes hand-in-hand with the freedom to assemble. These two are even listed in the constitution as if they were one and the same. During the Framers' lifetimes, the British government was not responsive to the needs or desires of the colonists. To the Framers, it was important that this did not ever happen again. In granting citizens the right to petition, they left the days of indifferent rulers in the past. Now, the government is expected to respond to the will of its citizens. Whereas a phone call only shows one person's care, a petition shows the government that there are many constituents concerned about the issue.

Not only are petitions powerful tools for the public, they are also very important to the government. It is the first responsibility of government to be responsive to what the people want. Phone calls and letters sent by one person are useful, but the organized coalition of concerned citizens in a petition show lawmakers that this issue is of concern to many. It is a useful mechanism to truly show congressmen which ideas are backed by popular sovereignty, and which are only of importance to a few people.

Although this freedom is not explicitly stated, the first amendment is what gives us the freedom to peacefully protest. A peaceful protest should be defined as anything that shows disapproval without the use of violence. This power is derived from the first amendment freedoms of speech, assembly, and petition. Assembly is the most important component from which we derive freedom to peacefully protest. Imagine the 1963 March on Washington without the freedom of assembly to protect the 200,000 protesters. If people could not come together to protest, change would not happen, at least not quickly. When peaceful protests take place, the government usually provides extra police protection, to ensure the safety of all involved. In the event that a peaceful protest turns violent, the police are there to stop any of those contributing to the violence. While it is entirely plausible for emotions to run high in this situation, the use of violence infringes on the right to peacefully protest.

Freedom of petition is the next most important freedom that constitutes peaceful protest. In a way, petitioning is a form of protest. In a petition, people sign their names to stand up for what they believe in, or put a stop to what they do not. While both freedom of speech and assembly lend themselves to make a component of the right to peacefully protest, only petition is something that can be used exclusively against the government. Speech and assembly play a part in our lives every day, and we usually do not use them for or against the government. Petitions are not a part of people's daily lives, nor do they use them except with the government. Protest is also something that people would probably only use against the government, except for labor unions that go on strike. In this way, the freedom to petition gives people the courage to take a stand directly against the government. Peaceful protest is the next logical progression when people feel emboldened enough to oppose the government.

Freedom of speech is vital to everything that we do, and protesting is no different. Because of freedom of speech, (also known as expression) people are free to support any cause that they choose, as long as they go about it in a peaceful manner. Without freedom of speech, there might be limits on what people could protest, even peacefully. Because of freedom of speech, people are free to act in favor of any cause that they believe in, even if it is not the popular sentiment of the time.

The first amendment is what protects all of our freedoms to express ourselves. This covers freedom of religion, speech, press, assembly, petition, and peaceful protest. Without these freedoms, the American people would not be able to shape the opinions of their lawmakers in the ways that they do now. Our first amendment rights are the most powerful tools we have to ensure that the government does not overstep its bounds.

References

1. Frank L Kidner, Maria Bucur, Ralph Mathisen, Sally McKee, and Theodore R. Weeks. "Making Europe: The Story of the West" (Cengage Learning, 2013) page 486
2. Adherents.com. "Religion of the Founding Fathers of America." N.p., n.d. Web. 21 June 2016.

Safeguards Against Tyranny (Amendments II- IV)

Whereas the very vast majority of Americans patriotically support the first amendment, the second amendment is more controversial. As a result of its brevity, the second amendment is often interpreted in many ways. Some argue that because the amendment states that the right of the people to bear arms will not be infringed, citizens should retain the right to keep as many guns as they want without controls by the government. However, there are many people that think that because the United States would never need to raise the state militias, more controls on weapons are needed. Many things factor into the interpretation of the second amendment: political attitudes, interpretation of the wording of the amendment, even how one interprets the comma in the middle of the amendment.

The Second Amendment reads, "A well regulated Militia, being necessary to the security of a free State, the right of the people to keep and bear Arms, shall not be infringed." The amendment can be construed in different ways because of the second comma. It raises the question, *do the people of the United States only have the ability to keep and bear arms for the purpose of maintaining the state militia?* When the Constitution was first outlined, state militias were the main source of military might in the United States. In the present time, there would be no reason that the United States would assemble a militia, rather than relying on the army. In fact, the state militia organization is now essentially obsolete. This means that if we are only allowed the right to own guns because of the state militias, gun ownership laws could be made much stricter.

It is up to the Supreme Court to interpret the Constitution, and the Supreme Court is very aware of the fact that the state militias are obsolete today. However, the Supreme Court has preserved the right of gun ownership to the people. But, this comes with restrictions. Convicted felons are not allowed to own guns in the United States, as they are viewed as too dangerous to retain this right. Furthermore, the United States requires background checks when somebody wishes to purchase a gun. Some people believe that background checks conflict with the Second Amendment, because they deny the right to bear arms to people who do not pass the check. Although virtually all people are against using guns to incite acts of violence, they are afraid of the Supreme Court limiting the Second Amendment, and therefore the Constitution.

It is the duty of the Supreme Court to ensure that the Constitution remains just as strong as it was upon its ratification. Although background checks help keep guns out of the hands of people that should not have them, they are not called for under the Constitution. And, although not many people are opposed to background checks, some are opposed to any practice that stands in the way of gun ownership. Furthermore, these people believe that background checks help the Supreme Court establish a precedent of putting barriers between the citizens and their guns. The most radical Second Amendment activists believe that background checks are just the first step in creating an entirely unarmed population.

So where should the second amendment stop? The Constitution has a precedent of ending peoples' freedoms when they begin to impede on the rights of others. It is not the ownership of guns that is dangerous to the right to life, it is people who abuse ownership of guns. Background checks are important to ensure that guns stay out of the hands of people who are likely to abuse them. Not only does this ensure the safety of those around them, it ensures their own safety.

According to the Center for Disease Control, in 2014, people were nearly twice as likely to kill themselves using guns than they were other people[1]. One of the other criteria that is used to determine whether or not someone can own a gun is mental health. Although some believe that mental health checks are a violation of the Fourth Amendment, they are a vital step in ensuring the right to life for everyone. Gun ownership is not necessary, it is something that people opt into. For this reason, it is treated as a privilege rather than a right. In order to obtain privileges in the United States, sometimes rights are offered in exchange.

In Rousseau's Social Contract, citizens give up freedoms in order to gain security from the government. This extends to gun control, because without governmental controls on gun ownership, anybody would be able to purchase a gun. Although most people could be trusted to govern themselves with a gun, it only takes one instance to ruin that privilege for everyone. People who wish to obtain the privilege of gun ownership trade their right to confidentiality of their mental health background. In doing this, the government is able to maintain their end of the social contract, as they are responsible for maintaining the safety of the people.

Today, whether or not Americans are better off, or safer as a result of the Second Amendment is debatable. However, we citizens have a duty to uphold our Constitution, and therefore, this amendment. In order to keep us safe, while also respecting our Second Amendment rights, the government does take certain precautionary measures. This further maintains the social contract between the people and the government.

And today, even though the state militias have been driven into nihility, the right of the people to bear arms has not been infringed. For people who live in more rural areas, or hunting aficionados, the right to bear arms is an important privilege. The government's efforts in ensuring that only responsible citizens can have guns is comparable to a walk across a tightrope. The government must straddle the line between being too loose with their standards, and being too controlling. In an ideal world, every gun owner would abide by the law, and nobody with malicious intent would be able to get a gun. This goal is largely unattainable, but with each gun control law passed, we get a little closer.

In an ideal society, gun violence deaths would be the exception, not the norm. Every year, more than 30,000 Americans die because of guns. Although we all know that guns are often the assisting party to murder cases, many people do not know that guns are used twice as often for suicide. Often, these suicide victims are excluded from the gun control narrative. The gun control debate often centers on homicide rates and violent crime statistics. The voices of those who have been silenced on their own accord cannot be ignored. Guns do not drive someone to commit suicide or homicide, but they are used as the mechanism to carry out this ultimate resolution. Depression, one of the leading causes of suicide, is a mental health issue. Mental health checks are vital to ensure that a person does not have the potential to be a danger to themselves. But, more important than mental health checks, is mental health itself. The only foolproof way to drive down suicide rates is to provide those in need with comprehensive mental health help and counseling.

The Second Amendment is as controversial as controversial an issue as any in this country. It is possible that if one canvassed the country, and interviewed all its citizens, no two people would be found who feel exactly the same way about the amendment. Standing in stark contrast to the controversy of the Second Amendment is the Third Amendment, which simply states that the quartering of soldiers is prohibited under times of peace, and must be approved in a manner prescribed by law in a time of war.

This amendment has never been the founding principal of a Supreme Court case, simply because there has never been an instance in the history of the United States where American soldiers tried to reside in someone's house. The United States does not often face war on home territory, especially not in the past 100 years. For this reason, soldiers are rarely in our presence. However, this amendment is important to maintain the rights to private property. One of the most important concepts enumerated in our Constitution is that private property cannot be taken without due process of law. The Third Amendment further protects property rights by ensuring that the government itself cannot seize property.

Although now this Amendment seems unimportant, it was very relative during the founding of our nation. One of the boiling points for relations between the British and the Americans was the

Quartering Act of 1765. This act required colonists to provide housing for the British soldiers in the colonies, which often meant keeping them in their own homes. In the divide between the Federalists and the Antifederalists during the founding, the Federalists had to assure the Antifederalists that the federal government would not be too powerful. This amendment is vital to that objective, because it maintains the all-important value of property rights, even against the federal government.

The Fourth Amendment continues to protect property rights beyond what the Third can. The Third Amendment protects an individual's right to their own home, while the Fourth protects essentially everything else beyond that. Beginning with the Fourth Amendment, the Bill of Rights transitions into talking about the rights that people retain if they have been accused of a crime. In the case of the Fourth Amendment, a person's property is protected from unwarranted search and seizure. The best example of the implementation of this measure is through the use of search warrants when someone has been convicted of a crime. In the United States, a search warrant can only be issued when probable cause is established. When a judge issues a search warrant, it is because they have probable cause to believe that the place for which the search warrant has been issued is connected to criminal, or otherwise illegal activity. Even when search warrants are issued, it does not give law enforcement the right to take anything and everything that they want; search warrants are issued for only specific purposes or items. For example, if a search warrant is issued to look for drugs, the search may not focus on guns. However, if illegal contraband is found during a search, it may be seized. This means that if a warrant were given to look for guns, drugs could be seized upon discovery.

This amendment also extends itself to intellectual property. The amendment states that "persons, houses, papers, and effects" may not be searched without probable cause and a warrant. As the world becomes more digitized, the concept of intellectual property becomes increasingly obscure. However, the groundwork for the security of our intellectual property is laid in the Fourth Amendment. The government may not seize the private property or papers of people without probable cause that a crime is occurring in relation to the place, property, or papers in question.

The Fourth Amendment is an important agent in making sure that the government does not seize too much power. Without the Fourth Amendment, the government would still have a means by which they could control the people without violating the First Amendment. If the government were upset with the actions of a private citizen, they would have the power to search and seize their personal effects, even if for no purpose other than simply being a nuisance.

For example, if the citizen publicly spoke out against the government, the government would be able to search the citizen's belongings, thereby incentivizing them to stop their criticism of the government. So although the First Amendment protects the right to speak freely, the Fourth Amendment takes away a device that the government might be able to use to limit free speech.

References

1. Kochanek, Kenneth D., Sherry L. Murphy, Jiaquan Xu, and Betzaida Tejada-Vera. "Deaths: Final Data for 2014." National Vital Statistics Reports 65.4 (2016): 30 June 2016. Web.

Rights of People and the Accused (Amendment V- Amendment VIII)

I plead the fifth. We hear this tired cliché in every crime show on television. In fact, we hear it so often, that we forget what the Fifth Amendment actually states. The fifth and sixth amendments of our Constitution combine to form the basis of our judicial system. One of the most important principals in the Fifth Amendment is that a jury of peers is necessary to make someone answer for a capital crime.

While we all know that the conviction of a jury is necessary to find someone guilty of a crime, not everybody knows that a grand jury is required by the Constitution to bring someone to trial for a "capital, or otherwise famous crime". The function of a grand jury is to determine whether or not there is probable cause to bring someone to criminal trial. Because this process was outlined in the Constitution, we can assume that it was important to the Framers. So then why don't all states use the grand jury process to indict someone with a crime? When the Framers wrote the Constitution- particularly the Bill of Rights- they expected that those principals would only apply to the federal government. This remained the case until Reconstruction. After the Civil War, and particularly after the Thirteenth Amendment was passed, the southern states tried to bar former slaves from the full protections of the law that white men were entitled to. Because of this, the Fourteenth Amendment was passed, which ensured equal protection under the law to all citizens, not only as citizens of the United States, but also as citizens of the state they lived in. Because of the protections that the Fourteenth Amendment establishes, the Bill of Rights could no longer be applied to only the Federal Government, but also to the states.

The Process of applying the Bill of Rights to the states is called *incorporation*. Supreme Court cases determine whether or not the rights that the citizens have against the federal government should also be safeguarded against the states. The Fifth Amendment has not been fully incorporated to the states. For this reason, the states do not have to assemble a grand jury to indict someone with a crime. In spite of this, many states still do use some kind of a grand jury system in order to charge defendants with serious crimes.

The next clause in the Fifth Amendment refers to what many Americans commonly know as "double jeopardy". This clause is the reason that O.J. Simpson is able to admit that he did in fact, commit the murders, without fear of having to stand another trial. Although in some cases, the double jeopardy clause allows guilty, dangerous criminals to walk away free, it protects our civil liberties. This part of the Fifth Amendment keeps the state from calling a defendant to repeatedly stand trial for the same crime. Imagine an America where the government had the ability to prosecute the same person over and over, until they finally got the verdict that they wanted. This darker version of America would deliver many innocent men and women into prison every year. Because of this clause, prosecuting attorneys are constantly under pressure to perform well, as they won't have another chance to go to trial.

To "plead the fifth" means that one is choosing to exercise their Fifth Amendment right not to incriminate themselves. Most importantly, this provision keeps trials honest. Although perjury is a felony, many people would likely lie in court in order to keep themselves from having to serve a lengthy prison sentence. If a jury is not given entirely accurate information, they will not be able to bring back a fully accurate verdict. The option to plead the fifth in a trial keeps legal proceedings honest and fair to both sides- and the jury. Furthermore, each trial has two sides. For our purposes, we will consider the Fifth Amendment in the context of criminal proceedings. In this type of law, there is the prosecution and the defendant. It should be entirely up to the prosecution to convince the jury of the defendant's guilt. If the defendant enters a plea of "not guilty," it should be entirely up to the prosecution to convince the jury otherwise.

Life, liberty, and the pursuit of happiness are the three concepts that Thomas Jefferson felt were paramount to protect in The Declaration of Independence. In the Fifth Amendment, the Framers state that life, liberty, and property cannot be taken away without due process of law. The writ of habeas corpus is a vital concept in American politics. During the Civil War, President Lincoln suspended habeas corpus and arrested several men whom he thought were impeding the union, its cause, and its army. To this day, the constitutionality of Lincoln's actions is debated. However one thing is certain, Lincoln's actions certainly would have been unconstitutional without the Civil War serving as their justification.

One liberty that all Americans enjoy is that we may not be detained without reason. Furthermore, all Americans have the right to know the charges for which they are being retained. The Fifth Amendment is the reason that the United States isn't able to arrest political prisoners whose only crime is their opinion. Journalists benefit the most from this concept. Without this constitutional protection, it would be easier for the government to incarcerate writers for publishing pieces that speak negatively of the government. While the First Amendment promises our rights to free speech, assembly, and press, the Fifth Amendment ensures it.

In terms of the judicial system, the Fifth Amendment ensures that the accused will receive a fair trial. The two words which best describe a fair trial are *competent* and *unbiased.* Competent refers to the court itself: the clerk, the judge, the prosecution, and the defense attorney. All of these people should be able to perform their jobs well and within the bounds of what is legal. The unbiased component of a fair trial refers to the jury. None of the jurors should walk into court with any preconceived notions about the case. Although there is much that goes into ensuring that a trial is fair, these two concepts are the most commonly cited when a verdict is appealed. Often, those found guilty try- and succeed- appealing based on the grounds that they did not receive a fair trial.

Finally, the last clause of the Fifth Amendment establishes that private property may not be taken away by the government without proper compensation. In some cases, the needs of the many outweigh those of the few. However, the Founding Fathers held the ownership of property and land in high esteem. For these reasons, the government must give adequate compensation to private citizens when their land or property is used in public works projects. This concept, called eminent domain, is the reason that we have public works such as the interstate highway system. Unlike the rest of the Fifth Amendment, this clause doesn't pertain to the individual during trial, but it still does protect their property rights. To the Framers, the right to hold property was nearly as important as the right to life itself. This is evident in so many of the great early documents in American history. In the Declaration of Independence, Thomas Jefferson stated that life, liberty, and the pursuit of happiness are among the unalienable rights endowed to all people by their creator. While the idea known as the pursuit of happiness can mean different things to everyone, it only meant one thing to the Framers: property. When the Constitution was ratified, property ownership was a qualification for suffrage. Often, the right to vote was synonymous with property ownership.

Together with the Fifth Amendment, the Sixth Amendment constitutes the fundamental aspects of the American justice system. The founding principal of the criminal justice system is (at least theoretically) that all are innocent until proven guilty. The Sixth Amendment maintains the rights of those accused of criminal offenses in the time between their arrest and trial.

The first promise that the Sixth Amendment makes is the right to a speedy and public trial. Going off of the condition that all are innocent until proven guilty, this provision is necessary to ensure that these people (who are still innocent before their trials) are not kept from their lives for too long. Furthermore, if a speedy trial were not guaranteed, the prosecution would have as much time as they want to collect their evidence and prepare their remarks against the defendant. Prior to the 1963 Supreme Court case *Brady v. Maryland,* the laws on what kinds of evidence the prosecution had to share with the defense attorneys were vague and varied from state to state. This meant that often, the accused and their attorneys would be unprepared to refute the evidence that the prosecution had against them.

The next clause of the Sixth Amendment states that the jury must be composed of citizens of the state and lawful district in which the crime took place. This is in keeping with ensuring that criminal trials are presented in front of a jury of peers. In the American political system, the judiciary is the only branch in which the citizens do not have a hand in election. American citizens do not elect federal judges nor Supreme Court justices. The trial by jury system was the mechanism that the Founding Fathers chose to employ in order to ensure that the citizens stay involved in all branches of government. However, the Founding Fathers did not come up with this system all on their own, like so many other constitutional principles, the trial by jury was inspired by the Magna Carta.

In a criminal trial, the prosecution presents their case against before the defense has the opportunity to present. This is because per the Sixth Amendment, those being tried have the right to know the nature and cause of the accusation against them. However, people know their charges long before their trial. Most people learn of their official charges upon arrest. While it is not required for the police to tell someone the reason for their arrest, this is generally what the police take it upon themselves to do. Legally, the accused must find out about their official charges either at an arraignment or at booking, depending on the nature of the arrest. If the arrest is a probable cause arrest, then the accused must hear their charges at an arraignment hearing. Usually this hearing takes place within two days of the original arrest. However, if the arrest was conducted with an arrest warrant, then the accused is presented with their charges sometime around their booking.

In any criminal trial, witnesses and their testimonies have the power to make or break the case against the defendant. In criminal trials, the accused has the right to be confronted with witnesses against him, as well as obtain witnesses in his favor. Because of the idea that all are innocent until proven guilty, it is the job of the prosecution to prove guilt, whereas it is the defense's job to maintain innocence. In order to maintain innocence, the defense and their counsel have the right to cross-examine the witnesses that the prosecution brings to the stand. The prosecution chooses their witnesses with the intent to prove the guilt of the accused.

Likewise, the defense brings witnesses to the stand that they believe will help maintain the innocence of the accused. This system of procuring witnesses is very evenly balanced to both sides. In order to maintain the doctrine of fair trial, this method of securing witnesses for testimony is necessary.

The provisions in the Sixth Amendment combine in order to form the basis for a fair trial in the American judicial system. However, the right to legal counsel is the most important right to ensure that the defendant has a fair chance to maintain their innocence. A trial cannot be considered fair if the prosecution comes armed with a team of lawyers, while the accused is left without counsel. If the accused cannot afford a lawyer, the state appoints a public defender to provide counsel to the defendant.

The 1963 Supreme Court case *Gideon v. Wainwright* established that the states must provide counsel to those that cannot afford it. In Gideon's case, the state of Florida had previously only offered counsel in capital cases. The Supreme Court unanimously ruled that legal counsel must be provided in all criminal cases. Solid legal advice is what best ensures that a trial is fair to both sides.

Whereas the Fifth and Sixth Amendments protect rights in criminal cases, the Seventh Amendment maintains rights in civil cases. Although the twenty dollar clause could now be considered outdated, due to the limited purchasing power of $20, the fundamental purpose of the Seventh Amendment is still important. Many of the concepts that are enumerated in the Constitution show us just how important property rights were to the Founding Fathers. The Seventh Amendment is a shining example of the importance of property rights, as it maintains the right to jury trial in civil cases.

As far as amendments go, the Seventh is relatively uncontroversial; its principals were incorporated into English Common Law long before the Framers wrote the Constitution. Simply, the amendment further incorporates citizens into the judicial branch, by allowing them to participate in a jury on a civil case. In doing this, the Founding Fathers extended due process of law to property. The twenty dollar clause is no longer the standard for civil litigations in federal courts, but interestingly enough, it is still the standard for some state courts. In actuality, the vast majority of civil cases that are tried at the state level are only tried by a judge, not a jury.

Furthermore, the Seventh Amendment also states that when a civil trial is concluded, it will not be re-examined in any court of law. This is the civil version of protection against double jeopardy. Whereas protection against double jeopardy keeps the defendant from being brought back to court until the state gets a favorable verdict, this clause in the seventh amendment prevents one side in a civil suit from bringing the other to court until a favorable verdict is reached. In a way, the Framers found a way to protect Americans from big corporations before such entities even existed. In a civil suit between a large corporation and a union, the corporation would have more financial resources to pay to keep going back to court. With all of these trials, the corporation and its legal counsel would have ample time to perfect their legal strategy, making a victory inevitable. However, the union would most likely exhaust its financial resources, and give up the cause before the corporation lets up.

Although all are innocent until proven guilty,

what happens when guilt is proven? In criminal trials, one common punishment is prison or jail time. However, the Founding Fathers did not turn their backs on those incarcerated Americans. Because of the Eighth Amendment, imprisoned Americans are granted humane treatment. Simply, this means that prisoners or those detained may not be tortured as a means of punishment.

One of the most contentious debates in all of our nation's history is whether or not the death penalty is a form of cruel and unusual punishment. The Fifth Amendment reads that among other things, life cannot be taken away without due process of law. Based on this assertion, it is safe to assume that the Founding Fathers believed that the right to life could be denied with due process of law. In fact, capital punishment has a rich tradition within English Common Law. Those who hold a more static view of the Constitution believe that the death penalty should be maintained in our criminal justice system, as it was an accepted punishment when the Constitution was ratified.

It is an error to only think of court proceedings whenever the United States judicial system is mentioned, as the corrections department is an extension of the crime and punishment system in the US. Because of their commitment to all facets of criminal justice, the Founding Fathers wrote the Fourth through Eighth Amendments to read almost like a story of conviction in the process of charging someone with a crime. The Fourth Amendment talks about the legal ways in which evidence can be obtained. In the Fifth Amendment, the Founding Fathers enumerated the rights that individuals maintain all the way up until their convictions. The Sixth Amendment follows, and outlines the guidelines that make up the criminal justice system in the United States. Although the Seventh Amendment deviates from the previous theme of criminal law, it is still essential for civil litigation. Finally, the Eighth Amendment returns us to the criminal justice system. After people are convicted of crimes, the Eighth Amendment ensures their bodily safety while incarcerated.

Jail time and prison sentences are not the quintessential version of the American dream, but all too often, they constitute the American experience. In fact, 9% of American men will spend time in jail. This figure is even higher for Hispanic and Black males at 16% and 28.5% [1] respectively. Because of the Eighth Amendment, the federal and state governments are not allowed to inflict cruel and unusual punishments onto prisoners. Obviously, as morals and ethics evolve with time, the idea of what is cruel and unusual changes.

In American society, the death penalty is often regarded as a cruel and unusual form of punishment. Many people cite the psychological effects associated with being sentenced to die. In many capital cases, the appellate process takes many years from start to finish. This causes psychological trauma as inmates wait for death, sometimes for years on end.

The death penalty has deep roots in almost every society. It outdates our nation, our government, and even democracy itself. While our idea of what is cruel and unusual will change with time, the implications of the death penalty will not. Perhaps a time will come when we do not use the death penalty as a punishment for the most severe crimes, but as of now, it is still constitutional.

References

1. Bonczar, Thomas P. Beck, Allen J. "Lifetime Likelihood of Going to State or Federal Prison." Bureau of Justice Statistics. March 1997. Web. 16 October 2016.

Ensuring Rights Not Listed (Amendments IX and X)

While writing the Constitution, the Founding Fathers ensured that the document itself would not be used to strip Americans of fundamental rights. Obviously, all of the freedoms that we enjoy as Americans cannot be expressed in only eight constitutional amendments. This shortcoming is rectified by the Ninth Amendment. Without the Ninth Amendment, the government would be able to deny the American people of any rights not clearly mentioned in the first eight amendments to the Constitution.

One such right is the right to privacy. Many Supreme Court cases are based on the fact that Americans are guaranteed privacy as an inalienable right. While we do enjoy privacy as a perk of being American, we often forget that privacy is not explicitly guaranteed by the Constitution.

The 1965 Supreme Court case *Griswold v. Connecticut* used the First, Third, Fourth, and Ninth Amendments as the basis to establish the right to privacy. The First, Third, and Fourth Amendments all put forth that American citizens may freely conduct their own affairs without interference from the government. The First Amendment allows speech, assembly, and worship to be kept away from the watchful eye of the government. The Third Amendment extends privacy to the home, keeping it safe from federal troops. However, the Fourth Amendment takes the right to privacy further than any of the other constitutional amendments. The very first clause of the Fourth Amendment states that people have the right to be secure in their persons.

This clause is worded in an obscure manner that allows for wide interpretation. In *Griswold v. Connecticut*, this clause allowed for the right to privacy to be codified. Americans have long enjoyed a great deal of freedom from the watchful eye of the government, however this right is not explicitly stated in our Constitution. It is only because of the Ninth Amendment that this principal can be incorporated into our rights without being written into effect as either a law or a constitutional amendment.

While we do not think of the final two amendments of the Bill of Rights as being vital to ensuring our inalienable rights, they The Ninth Amendment allowed Federalists and Antifederalists alike to rest easily knowing that the new federal government would not be able to take away the freedoms that people had enjoyed as colonists. The Ninth and Tenth Amendments acted as a bridge; they provided a common meeting point for delegates no matter their opinion on the role of federal government. Whereas the Ninth Amendment safeguards rights that lay with the people, the Tenth Amendment gives any powers not delegated to the Federal Government to the State Governments.

Often, we limit our scope of thought on balance of power to only the three branches of the Federal Government. In reality, the American political system is balanced in many ways, including between different levels of government. While it is true that if the Federal Government had more power there would be a lesser risk of disparity of rights and laws between states, it is also true that power concentrated at the Federal Level is both inefficient and tyrannical.

The United States covers a vast geographical area, and contains climates ranging from tropical to tundra and nearly everything in between. Also coming as a result of the vast area that the United States covers are the many different levels of urbanization. Because of these factors, lifestyles can vary greatly between states. Laws should always reflect the needs and values of the communities they serve, which means that laws are often different from one community to the next.

Year after year, gun control is the one of the most divisive issues in our nation. Liberals tend to view gun control as an issue of morality, whereas conservatives see it as an issue of upholding constitutional rights. Both sides of the debate believe that they are on the "right" side, albeit for different reasons. Although many factors play a role in shaping political sentiments, taking someone's geographic location into consideration can often provide insight into their opinions on a multitude of issues- including gun rigths. In rural areas, the concentration of conservatives tends to be higher than in urban areas. Supporters of gun rights can also be found more often in rural areas than in urban areas. In addition to rural residents being more conservative, they also have more need for guns. Those who live in rural areas are more likely to have jobs or hobbies that require guns.

In large cities, there are no large natural areas, predatory animals, nor game animals; people would be unlikely to buy guns for the purposes of hunting and defending against animal attacks. Although there are people from all walks of life that own guns for reasons of home security and self-defense, people in rural areas own guns for reasons that would not be valid in urban areas.

No state has "better" gun control laws than another, but every state has gun control laws that reflect the needs and values of its citizenry. Our nation boasts diversity as one its hallmark traits, however, with diversity comes different opinions, lifestyles, and needs. While states are often just as diverse as the nation itself, state legislatures are better able to reflect the needs of their citizens than the Federal Government.

State governments work in a closer proximity to their constituents than the Federal Government does. With this in mind, the Founding Fathers chose to add the Tenth Amendment to the Constitution.

These ten amendments to the Constitution are the most valuable weapons that Americans have to use against tyranny. While these amendments have been nearly set in stone since their ratification, they have been the subjects of many Supreme Court cases in the past 230 years. While Supreme Court cases cannot change the nature of the amendments themselves, they can change the way that the amendments are applied.

As more Supreme Court cases are held, the Amendments become more clearly defined. When the Bill of Rights was first written, it was supposed to be left open to different interpretations; this is especially true of the First Amendment. The Founding Fathers did not clearly define the parameters of what constitutes free speech because they did not believe that it would be beneficial to American liberties.

During the Founding Fathers' lifetimes, there were not many Supreme Court cases calling for one of the amendments in the Bill of Rights to be examined. However, the Revolutionary Generation passed on, and society has gotten increasingly litigious since. Because so many civil rights cases have gone through the American court system, the freedoms protected by the Bill of Rights have become rigidly defined. While these freedoms were never supposed to be so clear-cut, is it entirely a bad thing that they are?

Take into consideration the First Amendment right of free speech. Any government wishing to suppress its citizens must first take away freedom of speech in order to silence the opposition. It is for this very reason that the Framers did not want the government to play a role in determining the type of speech protected by free speech. The Framers believed that any freedom left to the people should not be subject to any interference by the government.

However, having clearly defined legal boundaries can also work to the citizen's advantage. Because of these well-documented expectations, citizens know what they are within their rights to do. Continuing with the previous example of free speech, precedent tells us that most forms of speech are protected unless they present a "clear and present danger." Furthermore, it is only because of court cases that the right to symbolic speech is protected. Without the right to symbolic speech, how would we know what we are allowed to burn? (Flags are okay, draft cards are not)

Although the First 10 Amendments to the Constitution have remained unchanged for more than 200 years, they are now incredibly cut and dry. While this wasn't the Framers' intent, this clarity came as a result of social progression. In the days of the Framers, these Amendments were supposed to be principals for citizens of a free democracy to follow, not articles destined to daily scrutiny and interpretation. However, it is only through this rigid nature that citizens may feel confident in expressing their rights, without fear of overstepping the boundary of constitutionality.

Economic Systems

Ultimately, the driving force behind any society is its economy. When the growth of an economy stops, the growth of its people do as well. Throughout human history, we have experimented with many types of economic systems, with some success and many failures. In the United States, our Republican system of government axiomatically makes some economic plans susceptible to failure before they can even be implemented.

In an egalitarian society, everyone has an equal opportunity to improve their lives; in a republic, every citizen has an equal opportunity to shape public policy. This belief in equality seemingly lends itself right into the iron fist of Marxist principles. Therefore we must ask: *In the United States, a nation which prides itself on equality, why will Marxism never work?* The answer is quite simple: the type of equality that most Western cultures believe in is *equality of opportunity.*

Equality of opportunity stipulates that everyone should be free from discrimination that may inhibit them from receiving the opportunities that everyone else gets. For example, in the United States, it is widely agreed upon that all children should have the opportunity to go to school and receive the same quality of education regardless of their race, gender, or socio-economic status.

By contrast, most Socialist or Communist nations believe in *equality of outcome.* A system based on equality of outcome is centered on the idea that all citizens should have their wants and needs fulfilled equally, regardless of how much effort they put into contributing to society. This means that one who drops out of school may lead a comparable life to a doctor, engineer, or other highly-skilled professional. In theory, Marxist systems are appealing because they promise that all people will have their basic needs met. While all people should feel secure in their abilities to provide for their families, American values dictate that income be determined by factors such as education and experience.

Because a society is driven by its economy, logic would tell us that the success of a society is, in part, determined by its economy. This is why the Founding Fathers believed so firmly in laissez-faire principals. In fact, one thing that has remained constant throughout all of American history is our belief in capitalism.

The complexities of Capitalism can best be summed up in two principals.

1. A capitalist economy is based on the free market and private ownership of the means of production

2. In a capitalist system, the government should have no interference with the free market

These two principals went unquestioned for over 100 years, until the presidency of Franklin D. Roosevelt. No economic crisis in the history of the United States cut as deep or as wide as the Great Depression. In previous economic depressions, the federal government provided little to no relief to struggling citizens. Previous financial crisis were left to be relieved by private charities and institutions.

Capitalist systems fluctuate constantly, usually, they are able to bounce back without extensive government intervention. During the Great Depression, the economy contracted so rapidly that bouncing back without government intervention was near impossible.

In a typical business cycle, the expansion period lasts considerably longer than the contraction period. At the onset of the Great Depression, it took only 21 months for the economy to reach a peak, and 43 months for it to reach a trough. After FDR began implementing his New Deal programs, the economy grew for a robust 50 months and contracted for only a marginal 13 months[1].

This drastic change in economic fluctuation is largely due to Roosevelt's bold action against the depression. While Roosevelt's actions helped the nation recover, they would have been disparaged by the Founding Fathers.

The Founding Fathers believed if the Federal Government were to have a hand in the economy, the government would become too powerful. Thomas Jefferson once espoused the belief that, "A government big enough to give you everything you want, is a government big enough to take away everything that you have."[2] Furthermore, many of the Founding Fathers were in favor of strong state governments and a weak federal government. Although the Articles of Confederation failed, many Antifederalists maintained their beliefs by joining the Democratic-Republican Party. Most importantly, this party believed in decentralized government.

When the Federal Government rolled out its New Deal programs, the balance between National and State governments shifted greatly. While state and local governments greatly assisted in the implementation of New Deal programs, the Federal Government was the ultimate authority. Before the Great Depression, the Federal Government was only relevant at war time and tax time, but after, the Federal Government came out omnipresent and nearly all-powerful.

Small state relief programs couldn't hold a

candle to the Civilian Conservation Corps, Public Works Administration, The Tennessee Valley Authority or the dozens other avenues for relief established by the Roosevelt administration. Furthermore, the New Deal made people increasingly dependent on the Federal Government for economic security. One of the most consequential programs from the New Deal was- and continues to be- Social Security.

Social Security allows older Americans to retire with the peace of mind that they will have a guaranteed income. Social Security provides incentive for older workers to retire so that younger workers can take their places. Social Security makes people more dependent on the Federal Government.

We've all heard the saying "don't bite the hand that feeds you," and this sentiment holds true when discussing Social Security. In part, the Founding Fathers were against public forms of welfare because of the dependence that it fosters.

Consider: older Americans vote in much higher numbers than younger Americans do. Any candidate that can win the senior citizen vote has a clear edge over the competition. One effective way to get the vote is to promise that more money will be awarded to seniors. Although Social Security payments are all but set in stone, promising to give seniors more money will surely entice them to vote for that candidate. While people in Democratic societies should always vote in their best interests, these campaign promises stretch this envelope greatly. The Founding Fathers were against government interference in the economy to begin with, and now we have made a whole campaign issue on it. How would the Founding Fathers feel about politicians openly promising a certain demographic money in exchange for their votes?

Guaranteed retirement income keeps money flowing in a Capitalist system. Furthermore, Social Security was deemed a human right by the United Nations Human Rights Council.[3] While this system greatly improves overall quality of life for American citizens, the Founding Fathers would abhor it.

Furthermore, the Great Depression also brought about incredibly expanded executive power. Article Two of the United States Constitution enumerates the powers that the President of the United States should and should not have. In reading Article Two, it becomes evident that the President is not meant to have the power to make laws. Rather than by a series of laws, the First New Deal was enacted by use of the executive order.

During the Great Depression, the country needed bold strokes, bold strokes that Congress could not produce. In choosing to enact his programs via executive order, President Roosevelt bypassed the process of finding a Representative and Senator willing to sponsor the bill, getting the bill through committee, getting the bill through both houses, and correcting any differences made to the bills in the houses. The process by which a bill becomes a law in the United States is quite lengthy (we all remember Schoolhouse Rock) and the country needed immediate relief.

By using executive orders, Roosevelt implemented his programs with the full force of law, while bypassing the extensive legislative process. Part of the President's executive duties is to, "take Care that the Laws be faithfully executed[4]." It is because of this duty that Presidents can issue executive orders. In order to issue a valid executive order, a President only needs to cite the law that he is helping to "execute". While all laws should be enforced to their fullest extent, Presidents often distort the original law in order to make their executive order lawful.

The Framers did not intend for the President to have this much power in implementing new programs. The Constitution does not grant the President the power of executive orders, nor does it explicitly mention any similar mechanism.

The New Deal left its mark on American society both economically and politically. The New Deal helped money flow more readily in an economy where spending money was not easy to come by. Along with expanding the economy, the New Deal also greatly expanded the role of the executive far beyond what the Framers would have wanted.

References

1. Public Information Office, "US Business Cycle Expansions and Contractions," *National Bureau of Economic Research, Inc.* 20 May 2016.

2. Thomas Jefferson Foundation, Inc. "Government big enough to give you everything you want...(Spurious Quotation)" *Monticello.* 20 May 2016.

3. United Nations Human Rights, "Toolkit on the Right to Social Security," *United Nations*, 22 May 2016.

4. US Constitution/ Article II, Section 3

Ecclesial versus Secular Interests

The United States was founded upon the principles of religious tolerance and freedom. Although it is evident that the United States is an ethnically diverse nation, it is also true that the United States is a religiously diverse nation. The separation of church and state allows for so many religions to coexist in the United States. In countries where religion provides the basis of law, religious conflicts are much more bitter and violent than nations that are not based in a belief system.

Although our government claims to be separate from all belief systems, we know that this was not the case when our nation was founded, and it is not entirely the case now. The government references a deity in many places: our currency, our pledge, our capitol buildings, and in nearly every speech made to the Bible belt by politicians. Although there is a high degree of separation of church and state in the United States, the break is not as clean as we might like to think.

In part, the intertwinement of church and state is due to the overwhelmingly Christian character of the United States. It is the responsibility of government to represent the population that it serves, often including in a cultural sense. Government and religion both represent the character and national values of a society, so it makes sense that the two are not mutually exclusive.

Our country's national motto is *In God We Trust,* which plays a large role in undermining the separation of church and state. It is only because of the statement's ambiguity that we do not consider it to be a clear violation of the separation of church and state. Supporters of this sentiment argue that it should be preserved because it does not make reference to any one god. Furthermore, this sentiment doesn't promote any kind of religious agenda.

Although the United States has been a Christian nation since the arrival of the pilgrims, a resurgence of religious fervor in the 1950's caused all of the theological allusions that we see in American society today. A notoriously god-fearing man, President Eisenhower signed into law a bill that required all US currency to bear the inscription "In

God We Trust."

Although we might believe that this saying has been a fixture of our society from the beginning, this law was only put into effect in 1955. While the vast majority of Americans at this time were Christians, the motto wasn't put onto money to reflect our culture, but rather to reject another one.

As tensions with the Soviet Union rose, Representative Charles Bennett proposed that faith set the United States apart from the "imperialistic and materialistic communism" of the Soviet Union[1]. Bennett believed that putting this symbol on currency would remind Americans that our material and economic prosperity was due, in part, to our spiritual faith. In keeping with the communist vs. capitalist rhetoric of the time, the saying was plastered onto currency. Nothing says capitalism quite like putting a national sentiment onto money.

The United States is commonly referred to as a "melting pot" of cultures; without the separation of church and state, this analogy would not be possible. The separation of church and states runs two ways: the government should be free of religious interests, and churches should be free of political influences.

Although this idea is more of an ideal situation than the actual American truth, there are several laws in place that require the government and religious institutions to occupy separate spheres. One such example is the 501(c)(3) tax exemption that makes churches and religious institutions tax exempt.

Although paying taxes does not seem like a radical way to keep church and state separate, this prevents secularization of churches. Citizens must pay taxes regardless of whether or not they agree with how their tax money is being spent. This is not the case for churches because they do not reap the same government benefits that citizens do.

In return for taxes, citizens receive several government programs and benefits that churches are simply not eligible for. One such example is free public education. Many religious institutions offer private education to members of their church.

For obvious reasons, religious schools are not given funding from the government. There have been numerous Supreme Court rulings and debates on the role that the government should play in funding and regulating religious schools. The Supreme Court case *Lemon v. Kurtzman* established a precedent for government involvement in religious schooling.

Religious schools cannot receive state funding, even to offset the cost of secular subjects. This case also established a precedent for all future legislation that required involvement from the church and the state. The aptly-named "Lemon test" gives three rules for laws that have the potential to mar the separation of church and state.

1. The statue must have a secular purpose
2. its primary effect cannot be to promote nor inhibit religion
3. It cannot result in excessive government

entanglement with religion

The Lemon test is a baseline mechanism to check for infringement of separation of church and state.

As with any area of legislation and regulation, there are grey areas that make the line between church and state fuzzy. Churches are a major agent of political socialization, which makes the line even fuzzier.

Members of the same church often vote the same way in elections. They hold the same values, which causes them to harbor the same political opinions. Often, clergy preach to their parishioners about issues that are at the forefront of American politics.

Churches have very strong feelings about issues like gay rights, abortion, and prayer in public schools. Many people of faith cite the bible as the reason for their opinions on these topics. More difficult to understand are those issues which religious people feel strongly about, but aren't rooted in scripture. The bible doesn't lend itself to issues like immigration, gun rights, and economics, but when we look at members of certain religious sects, their views tend to be very similar.

As previously mentioned, the separation of church and state isn't just a principle that the government must be cautious of; the church must also do their part. In a 2016 poll by the Pew Research Center, it was reported that nearly two thirds of American churchgoers surveyed had heard their clergy speak about political issues in recent sermons. Among the most-discussed issues were religious liberty, homosexuality, abortion, immigration, environmental policy, and income inequality[2]. Of these policy issues, religious liberty is the only one that directly affects freedom to worship. While people might feel strongly about the other issues as a result of their religious views, it is not the role of clergy to preach about them.

In order for a church to be a tax-exempt institution, it must stay out of the political realm. However important these issues may be, churches must refrain from preaching on them. Political views can be shaped through many avenues, including by the religious convictions that one holds. While beliefs and scripture might shape how one views the world, it is a violation of church and state for clergy members and institutions to capitalize on this.

People with similar beliefs (especially religious) tend to vote in similar manners. While this is a well-known idea, we must delve further into the reasons for this phenomenon. Members of a church all derive their moral from the same book and set of morals. While this provides a religious basis for political opinion, it is only when church authority attempts to influence views that the role of religion in political socialization is cemented.

Churches do important work in American communities every year; they provide food for the poor, shelter for the homeless, and do mission trips to impoverished areas across the globe. While religious institutions are important to millions of Americans, politics are equally as important. Politics and religion often complement each other, but this relationship is best when the two don't intersect.

The Fathers were not strangers to confounding the church and state. Some of the defining characteristics of our Constitution were based in Christian principle. The Founders used Christian morals to establish a secular society. While it seems antithetical to use religion as the base for a secular society, the founding fathers thought of the separation of church and state much differently than Americans do today.

As evidenced by influential documents from our nation's history, such as the Declaration of Independence, the Founding Fathers intended to keep god out of legislation, but not government itself. In the Declaration of Independence, Thomas Jefferson proposed that all men were endowed by their creator with certain unalienable rights. According to this line of reasoning, it is by virtue of the creator, and not by virtue of birth, that people have unalienable rights.

As proven in the above example, the Founding Fathers sometimes used religion as support for political ideas. Even Thomas Jefferson- notably agnostic- did so. The Founding Fathers believed that the separation of church and state meant that religious principles do not dictate law.

In societies that separate church and state,

any valid law is one which does not find its basis in religious text. The Framers intended this to be the guiding precept to keep religious and secular interests separate. As evidenced by the Declaration of Independence, the founders of our nation did not think that referencing a deity, even in important political documents, would intermingle church and state.

While today, the debate over state references to god rages, the Founding Fathers did not see it as a violation of the separation of church and state. As Americans continue to refine their definition of "the separation of church and state," the two will become increasingly distinct and independent.

As with any facet of society, shifting cultural values will continuously change the nature of church and state. While religion and politics are both important to the societies that they serve, they work best independently. The separation of church and state in the United States is what ensures that all citizens are equal under the law. Without this important principle, the United States would not truly be a democracy.

References

1. History, Art and Archives, The United States House of Representatives. "The Legislation Placing "In God We Trust" on National Currency." *United States House of Representatives Archives.* 19 March 2017.
2. "Many Americans Hear Politics from the Pulpit." *The Pew Research Center.* 2 April 2017. 28 September 2017.

Women in America

Before American independence was declared, Abigail Adams wrote a letter to her husband, John Adams, in which she urged him "I desire you would remember the ladies and be more generous and favorable to them than your ancestors"[1]. To this, John Adams responded with a sentiment akin to "don't be ridiculous[2]."

The status of women in America exemplifies just how far our nation has come since its founding. Women have always contributed to the prosperity of our country, but our country has not always contributed to the prosperity of women.

During the colonial period, the boycotts of British goods came down the hardest on women. Although many boycotts were organized by the Sons of Liberty, the burden of adjusting to the boycotts was often left to daughters. Women managed to adjust to the boycotts without sacrificing their qualities of life. Boycotts of British goods predate our nation itself, but if we move up the timeline, we find women contributing to the nation just as much as their male counterparts.

During the war for independence, British naval forces far outnumbered the few dilapidated ships that the colonies managed to scrape together. In Democratic societies, a war can only continue for as long as the citizens permit it. The British exploited this fact by using their naval strength to organize a blockade. The British blockade focused on port cities of high population. Cities like New York and Boston were of great importance to the colonists. Not only did many people live in these important urban centers, they were also important harbors.

The British blockade resulted in goods being unable to freely flow into the colonies. Families would have gone hungry if it weren't for the enterprising women of the time. In many cases, the men of the household left to go fight in the war, so women were left to looking after both the home and the family's crops. There are elements of this story that recur every time that the United States is involved in a major armed conflict.

In the First World War, women once again had to step into the roles that men left behind when they went to war. Not only did women fill the jobs that men left behind, they also had to fill new industries. During the war, women comprised the bulk of the munitions industry; when the war ended, so did their time serving the nation in this capacity. And while many women resumed their domestic duties at the war's conclusion, their impact would never fade from the American landscape.

World War One directly followed the Progressive Era, a time in United States history characterized by political reform and activism. One such form of activism was the women's suffrage movement, which was largely put on hold by WWI. When the war ended, so did the wait for suffrage. Through their wartime service, women had earned the right to vote. In August 1920, the Nineteenth Amendment was ratified, granting the right to vote to all citizens, regardless of their gender.

The history of women's rights in America started long before the suffrage movement, and will continue far into the future. First wave feminism was about gaining the right to vote, however, feminism did not die when that ends was achieved.

Feminism continued to evolve after the ratification of the Nineteenth Amendment. Although women could vote, they were still not equal under the law. Women were paid less than men for doing the same work. In order to ensure that men and women were equally protected under the law, Congress passed The Equal Pay Act of 1963.

This act ensures that any wage discrepancies between men and women are only a result of merit, seniority, or productivity[4]. While this law was a major victory for American women, there are many ways that employers could circumnavigate it. The most damaging of these ways are hiring terms that prohibit employees from disclosing their salaries to coworkers. While discussing money is taboo, it can be useful to do so with counterparts with the same job description. Discussing salaries allows employees to know if they are not receiving the same pay as their counterparts.

If a woman were being paid less than a male counterpart, she might never find out. In addition, an employee asking for a raise might not know how much to ask for without being allowed to consult coworkers. Employees cannot be expected to advocate for their rights if they do not know what they should be advocating for.

While the Founding Fathers were considered radical thinkers of their time, none of them believed in true equality of the sexes. To be fair to the Founding Fathers, they didn't believe in true equality of most people. When the Declaration of Independence was signed, only white, landowning men had the right to vote in twelve of the thirteen colonies (good on you, New Jersey[5]). In most states, women did not own the property necessary to vote. Some states allowed widowed women to own property, but even these women could not vote.

When women gained the right to vote, they still did not enjoy the full benefits of citizenship that men did. Part of citizenship means serving in the armed forces when the need arises. Women in the United States have a rich history of following around army camps to prepare meals, cook, and nurse the wounded. By World War Two, women became indispensable to the American military and its operations.

In WWII, around 140,000 women served in the Women's Army Corps[6]. Although these women did not serve in combat positions, their service was crucial to military operations. The mantra for women's service was "free up a man to fight." As long as women worked in intelligence, supply, administrative work, and similar positions, men did not have to. With fewer men needed in non-combat positions, more were available to fight.

Also in World War Two, women flooded to industrial jobs to support the war efforts. Although the Founding Fathers were not here to witness this, there is no doubt that they would have approved of women's conduct in WWII. As discussed in the economics chapter, the driving force of any nation is its economy. Before the Second World War, the American economy was predominately male. By entering into the workforce, women supported the economy throughout the war.

One thing that is true of all wars is how costly they are to fight. In order to support a war, a strong economy is needed. While the United States was fighting for independence, there was no Constitution, and therefore no way for the colonies to collect taxes as a whole. While we now consider the Continental Congress to have led the Revolution, this was not the case during the Revolution itself. Before the Constitution was signed, people considered themselves to be loyal to their state, rather than the country. The Federal Government had few ways to appropriate funds for Washington's army.

Because women in World War Two stepped into war industries, money continued to flow. When money flows, the government can continue to collect taxes, which allows funds to be allocated to war efforts. Without women, the economy would have become stagnant, making it difficult for the government to pay for the war.

Women helped in the Revolutionary war by following around army camps and maintaining farms. The farming industry was to Revolutionary America as the war industry was to World War Two America. These important industries allowed money to continue flowing, providing available capital to the government to use for war expenses. Capitalist systems are only able to work when money flows continuously. Without the contributions of women, the economy would have stalled before returning to productivity.

Women allowed the economy to stabilize in both of these wars by taking industries over from men. Without the contributions of women to keep the American economy afloat during wartimes, it is unlikely that the United States would be able to provide its army with resources.

While the Founding Fathers did not believe in gender equality, they did believe in effective governance. Although the Framers believed that property rights should be required for voting, it is a fact that most Americans now would not meet the property requirements. Although suffrage originally expanded to include white men that didn't own property, it took a while for non-property-owning women to be able to cast a ballot. In part, this was because the Founding Fathers believed that the ability to vote in the United States should be based partially on material wealth. Through hard work and service to their country, women were able to prove the Founding Fathers wrong. The basis of suffrage should be citizenship- not wealth.

References

1. History.com Staff. "Abigail Adams Urges Husband to 'Remember the Ladies'" *A+E Networks.* 12 July 2016.

2. David McCollough, *John Adams,* (New York City, USA: Simon & Schuster, 2001) page 105.

3. Paul S. Boyer, Clifford E. Clark, Jr. Karen Halttunen, Joseph F. Kett, Neal Salisbury, Harvard Sitkoff, Nancy Woloch, *The Enduring Vision: A History of the American People* (Boston: Wadsworth, 2011), pages 685-686

4. The Equal Pay Act of 1963. SEC. 206 [Section 6].

5. New Jersey State Constitution. Article IV. 1776.

6. "Women in the Army: World War Two" *Army.mil.* 27 July 2016.

Although today the United States is the foremost global superpower, our nation did not always have the influence that it currently does. While the United States now has a hand in nearly every country's affairs, it was not long ago that the United States was an isolationist nation. As the United States became increasingly involved in world conflicts, American influence expanded. Much can be discerned about the prosperity of a country from the way that it interacts with the other nations of the world.

When the United States first won independence, it did not have many dealings with other nations. The defeat of the indomitable British Army at the hands of the underprepared, undersupplied, and undertrained Continental Army sent shock waves across the world. Despite previous sentiments about American independence, other nations refrained from trade with the United States. Most nations were afraid of provoking the British by trading with its former colonies.

The most notable foreign ally of the United States was none other than France. Without French support during the War for Independence, it is unlikely that the colonists would have triumphed over the British. Out of gratitude for this instrumental support, America continued friendly relations with France- for a few years at least. America's isolationist spirit began when our support for France ended.

In 1793, France and Great Britain stood on the brink of war. Americans viewed this impending war as an opportunity to come to the aide of our greatest allies. Whereas citizens saw an opportunity to help a friend and further injure an enemy, the government saw possible consequences with disastrous connotations for the neoteric nation. Suppose the budding nation supported losing side of the war. *What would become of the hard-won independence that the nation had just come to know?* Rather than take the risk and stand by our allies, George Washington proclaimed neutrality in the conflict.

This decision by our first president set a precedent for similar situations. In its infancy, our nation didn't have the resources nor the capital to become involved in a European war. In the decades to come, France and Europe would further destabilize. President Washington sensed these first stirrings of violence as the prelude of larger conflicts to come.

Washington had correctly predicted the future instability in Europe. For many years, the entire European continent was engaged in constant struggle against power-hungry usurpers. Because of this instability in Europe, the United States lost many opportunities to introduce itself on the global stage. During this period of relative isolation, the United States followed Washington's neutrality proclamation.

It wasn't until Washington left the presidency that isolationist sentiment was cemented into the American political landscape. In his farewell address, Washington warned, "no entangling foreign alliances[1]." Although having allies, trading partners, and healthy diplomatic relationships with other countries is integral to the health of a nation, entangling alliances often do more harm than good.

The isolationist sentiments that Washington fostered during his presidency continued in future administrations. As the United States became more economically powerful, it had more global influence. One of the earliest examples of the United States getting involved in global affairs occurred during the Presidency of James Monroe.

Aptly named the Monroe Doctrine, these principles guided our nation during European attempts to meddle in the affairs of the Western hemisphere. Many Latin American countries began to declare their independence from Spain in the early nineteenth century. In the wake of the instability caused by independence, European countries- notably Spain and Portugal- tried to recolonize their former colonies.

The Monroe administration saw this European interference in the New World as dangerous to the balance of power across the American continent. The Monroe Doctrine took the United States from a position of isolationism to one of limited neutrality. The second declaration of the Monroe Doctrine continues the American tradition of neutrality. The Second Doctrine begins with a reminder that in all previous conflicts between European nations, the United States maintained a position of neutrality. The doctrine also recounts that during the Latin American revolutions, the United States remained neutral.

The thread of neutrality and isolationism that characterized United States foreign relations for previous decades began to unravel with the Monroe Doctrine. Although the United States had maintained neutrality up to that point, the Monroe Doctrine decreed that any European attempts to control the newly-independent Latin American republics would be viewed as, "the manifestation of an unfriendly disposition towards the United States."

The Monroe Doctrine was significant because it was the first major foreign policy proclamation that showed American willingness to become involved in international conflict. While our nation continued to keep to itself, the end of the nineteenth century marked a turning point for American foreign policy.

Although the Monroe Doctrine was written in 1823, the Spanish-American War in 1898 was the first time that the United States went to war with a European power over involvement in the Western Hemisphere.

The Cuban struggle for independence from Spain tugged at the heartstrings of many Americans who drew parallels between the Cuban and American revolutions. While this sentiment sparked the earliest cries for the United States to assist the Cubans, the mysterious explosion of the U.S.S. Maine in Havana Harbor ultimately catalyzed United States involvement in the struggle for independence.

This "splendid little war" -as it was called by Ambassador John Hay in a letter to Theodore Roosevelt- resulted in the United States acquiring the Philippines, Puerto Rico, Guam, and nearly Cuba. Although the United States and Spain both recognized Cuban independence after the war, the United States kept a close watch on the affairs of the island nation for years to come.

The Spanish-American War was the first major conflict that the United States got involved in that didn't directly involve the United States. Although the sovereignty of Cuba would have impacted the United States, the United States was not a party in this conflict until it made itself so.

The Spanish-American War was just the first in a long-and continuous- string of conflicts that the United States would meddle in. The next such conflict was none other than the First World War.

Still avidly isolationist, the United States refrained from involvement in World War One for as long as possible. As soon as it was apparent that the outcome of the war would have great consequences for the world, the United States entered the conflict on the side of Great Britain, France, and Russia. Although Woodrow Wilson ran his reelection campaign on the idea that he had kept the United States out of the war, aggressive actions by Germany made American entrance into the war inevitable.

The most damning action by Germany was what is now known as the "Zimmermann telegram." This telegram was sent from Germany to Mexico in January 1917; it promised that if Mexico declared war on the United States, Germany would help Mexico regain the territories of Arizona, Texas, and New Mexico.

After the victory of the entente powers in World War One, the United States was given the opportunity to help negotiate the terms of peace. More important than this chance was the global prestige that came with winning a global conflict. The United States had proven itself to be a valuable ally to the most formidable powers in Europe.

World War One marked the end of isolationist

sentiments in the United States. In global conflicts to come, the United States would take decisive actions early on.

While the First World War put the United States in a position of global power, it was not until after the Second World War that the nation would be considered a global superpower.

After the defeat of the Axis powers, Great Britain, the Soviet Union, and the United States firmly established their positions at the top of the global hierarchy. While Great Britain enjoyed the standing that came from hard-earned victory, their domestic financial situation prevented them from being as influential as the United States and the Soviet Union. The reconstruction of war-torn areas was carried out predominantly by the United States and the Soviet Union.

The reconstruction efforts took place during the Cold War; some of the nations under reconstruction (Germany, Korea, and Vietnam, to name a few) were the host sites of a few satellite wars of the larger Cold War.

When the Soviet Union finally fell, the United States could definitively claim to be the most influential country on earth.

Another development that came out of the Second World War that solidified America's global prominence was the United Nations. As a founding member of the United Nations, the United States has privileges that regular members do not. The United

States has a permanent seat on the UN Security Council- a perk that also comes with veto power. The United Nations gives the US an opportunity to maintain peaceful diplomatic relations with the world.

Foreign relations are shaped by diplomacy and economics equally. The forces of supply and demand can be just as important in forging foreign relations as the forces of war and peace. The United States accounts for a quarter of the world's GDP[2], making our nation the largest economy in the world. The incredibly prodigious economy of the United States is a tool which the United States can use to influence other nations.

While this is not economic imperialism, it might be referred to as "economic influencing." To lose the United States as a trading partner would be to lose a quarter of the world's trading opportunities. The United States is fully aware of this, and uses it to its fullest advantage.

There is no better example of the Unites States using trade as an arm of foreign policy than in Cuba. Cuban-American relations have been icy for several generations, a trend that we are only now starting to break. The most recent presidential administrations have gradually loosened trade restrictions with Cuba. Along with the loosening of these trade restrictions came increased friendliness between the two nations. As trade restrictions were loosened, sentiments between the two nations became more pleasant, and as sentiments became more pleasant, more trade restrictions were loosened. While one event does not directly trigger the other, the two work hand-in-hand to complement each other.

The first major step in freeing trade between the two nations was the Trade Sanctions Reform and Export Enhancement Act of 2000. This act allowed for exports to be sent from the United States to Cuba in the agricultural and medical fields[2]. While exports are not necessarily synonymous with trade, this milestone marked a turning point for Cuban-American trade relations. Since this initial easing of trade restrictions, the United States has taken several steps towards more open trade with Cuba.

Since our nation has been independent, it has had to deal with other sovereign nations. In the beginning, the United States did not have much interaction with other nations, with the exception of only the most necessary trade. It was only when American interests were threatened that the United States began to get involved in global affairs. Despite the strict isolationism that characterized national character for the first half of our nation's existence, the World Wars offered the first opportunity for the United States to promulgate itself onto the global stage.

The development of the United States as a nation can be effectively tracked through its foreign policy decisions. The progression of the United States from a timid state to a confident empire can be clearly observed. Although President Washington warned against entangling alliances when he left office, in today's incredibly interconnected world, alliances are a necessity. Washington would no doubt be shocked by concepts like the United Nations, free trade agreements, and international law, but we can't know that he would have disapproved of them. During Washington's time, these concepts had not yet been dreamt up- and for good reason.

Communication between nations took months, especially for the United States, which was separated from the Old World by an ocean. This lack of contact with other nations fostered the isolationist sentiments that characterized American foreign policy for upwards of 100 years. Today, communication is all but instantaneous, which leads to increases in the amounts of correspondence between nations. More communication and interaction between nations also brings the opportunity for more conflicts. This is why global entities like the United Nations are necessary today.

Changes in foreign policy must be made in order to ensure a nation's success in an ever-changing world. Although American foreign policy has changed considerably since our nation's infancy, it has done so in a way that has stayed true to American character.

References

1. George Washington, "Washington's Farewell Address" (1796), in *Great Debates in American History: Foreign Relations, Part I*, ed. Marion Mills Miller (New York: Current Literature Publishing Company) Pages 58-68.

2. The World Bank. "GDP (current US$)." *World Bank Group.* 2016. 12 July 2017.

3. Department of the Treasury. "Trade Sanctions Reform and Export Enhancement Act of 2000 (TSRA) Program." *The United States Department of the Treasury.* 15 July 2017.

Conclusion

The American experience is unlike that of any other country in the world. Our nation is still in its infancy, taking its first steps towards some unknown destiny. However, our young nation is currently governed by the world's oldest constitution. It seems almost paradoxical that our Constitution, at just over 200 years old, is the oldest codified model of government that the world has to offer.

Back in 1630, John Winthrop proposed that New England should consider itself to be a city on a hill: a model to be observed by the eyes of the world. Nearly 400 years later, the United States has become a shining example of governance for the rest of the world.

Also unique about the American experience is that there are endless ways to tell the American story. Let us not forget that the United States was established by immigrants from Britain. In this way, the first Americans were not American at all. Our nation was built on the backs of those that crossed oceans in search of a better life- and on the backs of those who were forced to cross oceans without their consent. The American experience cannot be homogenized down to only one race, one gender, one religion, or even one country of origin.

The American experience escaped religious persecution in Great Britain; the American experience fled famine in Ireland; the American experience came from China to mine for gold in California; the American experience crossed the border from Mexico. It is only in this nation that these diverse experiences can come together cohesively.

The very nature of the American political system allows for all of these diverse perspectives to be represented. While the citizens are given plenty of opportunities to shape the fate of the nation, they must take it upon themselves to actually do so. Political activism begins with understanding the nature of our charter of government. Although we are governed by the world's oldest written constitution, much has changed since our Constitution was ratified.

All of these changes can be easily tracked and understood, but it is up to us to decide the route that our nation will take in the future. This is why a well-educated citizenry is so important. As our nation evolves, we must look toward the future while keeping the past in mind. The city on a hill has come a long way from where it was in 1630. The distance to which we can take the American experiment depends on how much we learn from history.

In our history as a nation, we have put many policies into effect, with some successes and many failures. To look towards the future is also to look into the past and analyze what we did right and why. On a fundamental level, this begins with the Constitution. Our most important document outlines the entire plan for our federal government; it deserves our full understanding.

Now, we are not just a city on a hill, but a nation on a mountaintop. Without the changes that we have made to our Constitution, we would have slipped from our peak a long time ago. If a country cannot keep up with the changes around it, it is destined to be left behind.

"The Constitution is the guide which I never will abandon"

-George Washington

A Note from the Author

Some authors are simply born with the ability to churn out pages upon pages of product a day; I am not one of those authors. I began to write this book about four months before my sixteenth birthday, although on a completely different trajectory. Originally, my goal was to write a long essay about feminism and its relationship with the political culture of the United States. Painstakingly, I wrote my first manuscript of this essay by hand in a composition notebook. However, as I began to type up my work, I began to deviate from what I had written. After a few weeks, I had typed upwards of twenty pages about what I believed feminism should encompass.

For several months after this, I felt as though I had hit a brick wall. Writers' block is most certainly alive and well, and I felt it weighing down on me during the following months. Finally I came to the conclusion that the best thing for my creative faculties would be to delete the essay that I had written. Anyone who knows me personally knows that I am not an impulsive person, however I deleted that essay without a second thought.

In the end, deleting that essay turned out to be the best choice that I could have possibly made. My mistake was writing about feminism and American political culture as if they were mutually exclusive. I feel as though this is a mistake that many others have made when writing about American politics and government. So much of American history is told through the eyes of men, simply because women have been left out of the conversation for so long. Because men dominate American history, we assume that the American experience is male. More so than anything, the American experience is female. Overwhelmingly, America's course has been charted by men, while women are left to be swept by the current.

In the entire course of our nation's history, men have had the ability to legislate, create, think, and rule. The only power that women have retained throughout all of U.S. history is the ability to experience. Women have been the silent sufferers from the founding of our nation up to the present. Their experiences constitute what it really means to be an American. Their experiences are those of sacrifice, of strength, of love, of loss, and of patriotism.

I don't know how my essay about feminism

became a book about Constitutional change, but I'm glad it did. When we understand the framework for a country's government, we understand the values that the country holds. Over time, our interpretation of the Constitution has changed as a result of our ever-changing values. Because our values have changed, we have expanded suffrage to include non-landowners, racial minorities, and yes, women.

If the Framers were alive today, they would no doubt shake their heads at some of the laws, programs, and customs that we have today. However, I don't think they'd be disappointed. Society and technology have advanced so far since the Revolutionary era that law must evolve too so as to keep up. In fact, law unable to keep up with the needs of society is unfit to govern a nation.

The laws that governed the Revolutionary Generation were the most appropriate laws for that time. Now, our laws are the most important to govern our society today. While looking at any changes in the interpretation of law, one must consider the needs of that nation.

In and of itself, change is neither bad nor good. Change can happen for the better, and change can happen for the worse. As citizens, it is our job to ensure that change in our nation is always positive. As time marches on, we should strive to keep up.

Works Cited

Adalian, Rouben Paul. "Turkey, Republic of, and the
Armenian Genocide." *Armenian National
Institute*. N.D. Web. 6 March 2016.

Adherents.com. "Religion of the Founding Fathers of
America." N.p., n.d. Web. 21 June 2016.

Bonczar, Thomas P. Beck, Allen J. "Lifetime Likelihood
of Going to State or Federal Prison." *Bureau of
Justice Statistics*. March 1997. Web. 16 October
2016.

Boyer, Paul S. Clark, Clifford E. Jr. Halttunen, Karen.
Kett, Joseph F. Salisbury, Neal. Sitkoff, Harvard.
Woloch, Nancy. *The Enduring Vision: A History
of the American People*. Boston: Wadsworth,
2011.

Congressional Budget Office. "Updated Estimates of the Effects of the Insurance Coverage Provisions of the Affordable Care Act, April 2014." *Congress of the United States Congressional Budget Office.* April 2014. Web. 29 December 2016.

"Congressional Voting Turnout Is at Lowest Mark Since 1978." *The United States Census Bureau,* 16 July 2015. Web. 04 Jan. 2017

Department of the Treasury. "Trade Sanctions Reform and Export Enhancement Act of 2000 (TSRA) Program." *The United States Department of the Treasury.* 15 July 2017.

The Equal Pay Act of 1963. SEC. 206 [Section 6].

"The Executive Branch." The White House. N.D. Web. 22 January 2017.

"The Executive Branch." *The White House. The United States Government,* 01 Apr. 2015. Web. 31 Dec. 2016.

The Federal Election Commission. *Federal Election 94: Election Results for the U.S. Senate and the U.S. House of Representatives.* Washington D.C. 1995

"Federal Elections 2012: Election Results for the U.S. President, the U.S. Senate, and the U.S. House of Representatives." FEDERAL ELECTIONS 2012 (2013): n. pag. *Federal Election Commission.*

Fitzgerald, Sharon C., Daily Progress Correspondent.
"Survey: U.S. Admires, but Hasn't Read,
Constitution." *The Daily Progress*. N.p., 23 Jan.
2013. Web. 12 February 2016.

"Gideon v. Wainwright." United States Courts. N.p., n.d.
Web. 25 Mar. 2017

"Griswold v. Connecticut." *Oyez*, Accessed 31 May. 2017.

The Gun Control Act of 1968 Title 18, United State Code,
Chapter 44, §101- §924 (1968).

Hamilton, Alexander. "Federalist No. 78." *The Federalist
Papers*. 28 May 1788. Accessed via web. 17
September 2017.

Hentoff, Nat. "Our Constitution: How Many of Us Know
It?" *Cato Institute*. N.p., 19 May 2011. Web. 12
February 2016.

History, Art and Archives, The United States House of
Representatives. "The Legislation Placing "In God
We Trust" on National Currency." *United States
House of Representatives Archives*. Web. 19
March 2017.

History.com Staff. "Abigail Adams Urges Husband to
'Remember the Ladies'" *A+E Networks*. Web. 12
July 2016.

Hooper, Laural L., Jennifer E. Marsh, and Brian Yeh.
"Treatment of Brady v. Maryland Material."

United States Courts. Oct. 2004. Web. 25 Mar. 2017.

Kidner, Frank L, Maria Bucur, Ralph Mathisen, Sally McKee, and Theodore R. Weeks. "Making Europe: The Story of the West" (Cengage Learning, 2013)

Kochanek, Kenneth D., Sherry L. Murphy, Jiaquan Xu, and Betzaida Tejada-Vera. "Deaths: Final Data for 2014." National Vital Statistics Reports 65.4 (2016): 30 June 2016. Web.

"Many Americans Hear Politics from the Pulpit." *The Pew Research Center.* 8 August 2016. Web. 2 April 2017.

"Marbury v. Madison." Primary Documents in American History. *Library of Congress,* n.d. Web. 5 March 2017.

McCollough, David. *John Adams.* New York City, USA: Simon & Schuster, 2001.

New Jersey State Constitution. Article IV. 1776.

Obama, Barack. "Healthy Communities Reward Speech." 3 March 2016. Milwaukee, WI.

Public Information Office, "US Business Cycle Expansions and Contractions," *National Bureau of Economic Research, Inc.* web. 20 May 2016.

"The Senate's Role in Treaties." The United States Senate.

N.D. Web. 3 January 2017.

Thomas Jefferson Foundation, Inc. "Government big enough to give you everything you want...(Spurious Quotation)" Monticello. 20 May 2016.

United Kingdom Parliament Act of 1911. 1911.

United Nations Human Rights, "Toolkit on the Right to Social Security," *United Nations*, web. 22 May 2016.

The United States Census Bureau. "Annual Estimates of the Resident Population: April 1, 2010 to July 1, 2016." *The United States Census Bureau*. July 2016. Web. 30 December 2016.

U.S. Constitution/ Amendment 1

U.S. Constitution/ Amendment 2

U.S. Constitution/ Amendment 3

U.S. Constitution/ Amendment 4

U.S. Constitution/ Amendment 5

U.S. Constitution/ Amendment 6

U.S. Constitution/ Amendment 7

U.S. Constitution/ Amendment 8

U.S. Constitution/ Amendment 9

U.S. Constitution/ Amendment 10

U.S. Constitution/ Amendment 13

U.S. Constitution/ Amendment 14

U.S. Constitution/ Amendment 19

U.S Constitution/ Article I, Section 7

U.S. Constitution/ Article II, Section 2

U.S. Constitution/ Article II, Section 3

U.S Constitution/ Article III

U.S. Constitution/ Article IV

U.S. Constitution/ Preamble

"Vetoes: Summary of Bills Vetoed, 1789-present" *The United States Senate.* N.D. 1 February 2017.

"Voting within Australia – Frequently Asked Questions." *Australian Electoral Commission.* N.p., 27 Oct. 2016. Web. 13 June 2016.

Washington, George. "Washington's Farewell Address." 1796. In *Great Debates in American History: Foreign Relations, Part I.* Edited by Marion Mills Miller. New York: Current Literature Publishing Company. 1917.

"Who Votes? Congressional Elections and the American Electorate: 1978–2014." *Census Bureau.* July 2015. Web. 13 June 2016.

Wilson, Megan R. "Lobbying's Top 50: Who's Spending Big" *The Hill.* 7 February 2017. Web. 28 May 2016.

Wilson, Reid. "Only 36 Percent of Americans Can Name the Three Branches of Government." *The

Washington Post. 18 September 2014. Web. 27
February 2016.

"Women in the Army: World War Two" Army.mil. N.D.
Web. 27 July 2016.

The World Bank. "GDP (current US$)." *World Bank
Group.* 2016. Web. 12 July 2017.

"2016 Leadership PACs and Sponsors." Federal Election
Commission Leadership PACs and Sponsors RSS.
Federal Election Commission, n.d. Web. 04 Jan.
2017.